The Accidental Adventurer

THE ACCIDENTAL ADVENTURER

MEMOIRS OF THE FIRST WOMAN TO CLIMB MOUNT McKINLEY

BARBARA WASHBURN

WITH LEW FREEDMAN

EPICENTER PRESS

To my children Dotty, Teddy, and Betsy, and to my husband, Brad,
my guide who made me an "accidental adventurer."

Text © 2001 Barbara Washburn
Photos from the collections of Bradford and Barbara Washburn unless otherwise credited

Publisher: Kent Sturgis
Editor: Don Graydon
Proofreader: Sherrill Carlson
Designer, production: Jennifer LaRock Shontz
Mapmaker: Jennifer LaRock Shontz

Front cover photographs: *Kahiltna Dome, Mount McKinley; Barbara Washburn on the summit of Mount Bertha;* (Both photos courtesy of the National Geographic Society) Photo collage by Jennifer LaRock Shontz.
Back cover photograph: *Barbara and Bradford Washburn after the first ascent of Mount Bertha on July 30, 1940.* (Courtesy of the National Geographic Society)
Frontispiece: *Barbara Washburn running a sled behind dogs on the Brady Glacier during the Mount Bertha climb in 1940.* (Courtesy of the National Geographic Society)

ISBN 978-0-945397-91-5

10 9 8 7 6 5 4 3 2

Library of Congress Catalog Card Number: 00 136170

Epicenter Press Inc. is a regional press founded in Alaska whose interests include but are not limited to the arts, history, environment, and diverse cultures and lifestyles of the North Pacific and high latitudes. We seek both the traditional and innovative in publishing nonfiction trade books and gift books featuring contemporary art and photography.
To order single copies of THE ACCIDENTAL ADVENTURER, mail $16.95 (softbound edition) [Washington residents add $1.47 sales tax] plus $5 for Priority Mail shipping

CONTENTS

PREFACE

BARBARA WASHBURN WAS A NAME for me before she was a face.

Any student of Alaskan mountaineering is familiar with Barbara Washburn as the first woman to climb Mount McKinley. In 1947, when it was virtually unheard of for a woman to be included on a major mountaineering expedition, she authored an indelible piece of climbing history.

Of course, the name Washburn is one of the most esteemed in Alaska climbing annals, anyway. Barbara's husband, Bradford, has long been regarded as the most knowledgeable expert on McKinley and was involved in three early ascents of the peak.

Brad and Barbara became a husband-and-wife climbing team in the 1940s and literally put unknown Alaskan places on the map: When they weren't climbing, they were mapmakers. While always making their home in Massachusetts, the Washburns became famous adopted Alaskans.

Beginning in the 1980s, through my job as sports editor of the *Anchorage Daily News,* I had the opportunity to write many stories about mountain climbing. I initially developed a friendship and working relationship with Bradford Washburn. And through Brad, of course, I met Barbara, both on their regular excursions to Alaska and on my own trips back to the Boston area, where I grew up.

Barbara Washburn is not a boastful woman. I learned the most about her Alaska adventures by reading expedition diaries tucked away in archives at the University of Alaska Fairbanks. Her climbs of Mount Hayes and Mount Bertha may be overshadowed by her singular accomplishment in scaling McKinley, but they, too, are notable achievements, both of them first ascents.

On the fiftieth anniversary of Barbara's ascent of McKinley, the Washburns returned to Alaska for several celebratory events. What a delight it was to listen to Barbara recount the climb from the vantage point of five decades later. During a conversation she mentioned that she had attempted to write an autobiography for her children only.

Some time later she offered me the chance to read what she had written and I was captivated. Barbara Washburn has led an exciting and admirable life, fulfilling many roles: mother, wife, teacher, mountaineer, surveyor, world traveler. In 1999 we began working together to expand and fine-tune this little autobiography.

Barbara has garnered numerous honors from prominent organizations, yet has never lost her New England, down-home modesty. She would be the first to argue that her life at the center of high adventure was partly happenstance, a fortuitous gift of fate. Luckily, I had both the opportunity and responsibility to draw her out and help her put her thoughts and experiences down on paper. This book is the result: The story of a woman who was born with a brave heart and let it guide her through a lifetime of spirited endeavor.

— *Lew Freedman*

Mount McKinley stands 20,320 feet high—highest of any mountain in North America.

Introduction

THE VIEW ALL AROUND WAS TRULY THE WAY I imagined heaven to be when I was a little girl. All puffy clouds. An endless horizon. Just the way a kid would picture it.

I stood on the roof of North America, the summit of Mount McKinley. I was very cold. The wind was gusting to thirty miles an hour and the temperature was twenty degrees below zero. No matter how bundled up I was in a thick, protective parka, and no matter that the calendar read June, I was cold. And I knew I would be there for a while because our climbing party had survey work to do.

I tried to keep from freezing by wiggling my hands and by jumping up and down. At the same time, I did my best to absorb the view. I would probably never have the chance again.

What was I looking at? Just about all of Alaska.

It was June 6, 1947. Our expedition was only the fourth to ever achieve the summit of McKinley, at 20,320 feet the tallest mountain on the continent. I was the first woman to climb the mountain, but my thoughts were less on history than on preserving my body heat—less on posterity than on getting back down safely.

In the moments before we reached the summit, it became apparent that some of the others in our group had a greater sense of the significance of the occasion than I did. On the summit ridge, I was roped to Bill Hackett and Shorty Lange. My husband, Bradford Washburn, the leader of the expedition, had just unroped from us. We kept climbing as he dropped back a bit to take pictures.

I had become exhausted as we climbed ever-higher in the thin air. Then I got a second wind, and only a short way from the summit I felt that I really might make it. Bill was not feeling well. He leaned on his ice axe, suffering from a headache. I was sympathetic, but I had to keep moving because Shorty was pulling me forward.

Just as we approached the last steps to the summit, Shorty stepped aside and said, "You go first. You're the first woman to stand on the summit of the highest peak in North America!"

That sounds pretty dramatic, but at that moment the accomplishment did not seem very important to me. Still, this was not the place for an argument. But just as I stepped forward, I felt a jerk on the rope and I almost lost my balance. Startled, I looked back and saw Bill struggling for breath, leaning head-down on his axe.

Forgetting politeness, I yelled, "Let me go! I have to move forward!"

Bill released me, then regained his strength and walked up to us. We stepped forward together as we figured out which of the several little rock-hard snow mounds was the true summit. Soon other members of the group joined us on top.

I recalled then what Robert Tatum, a member of the first party to reach the summit, had said about the view: "It was like looking out the windows of heaven."

Before me lay more than 100,000 square miles of Alaska. Snow-covered mountains and terrain stretched to the horizon in a view that left me breathless. There were no windows, however, no buffer between my body and the cold, so it took all of my focus to work at fighting the cold. I kept telling myself that I must keep my head clear and be prepared for the difficulty of the descent. I had to get home to Massachusetts and our three young children.

It was strange that I should find myself in this place at all. I had never dreamed of becoming a mountaineer. It had not been my plan to climb Mount McKinley—and certainly not a goal to be the first woman to stand on its summit. It sometimes seemed that it had all happened by accident.

But there I was. Many other women may have wanted to do it before me but never had the chance. The world was a very different place in 1947 than it is now, when women have so many more opportunities and career options. It would be nice to say that I considered myself to be a pioneer and that I wanted to climb Mount McKinley to prove something for all women. But that would not be true. I did not think that way.

To be perfectly honest, the main reason I wanted to go to Mount McKinley was that my husband was going and I wanted to be with him. That was perfectly logical thinking back then. I did not feel I had anything to prove.

It was wrenching to leave our children behind, even in the care of relatives, and I was worried the entire trip that something would happen to them while I was away. I would feel guilty forever. But once I became a part of the expedition, I decided to make the most of it. I very much wanted to reach the summit, and as the only woman I felt a certain pressure to succeed. I had to show that I could do it.

I was not a highly trained mountaineer when I traveled to Mount McKinley, though I had already been on two earlier Alaska climbs with Brad. He had always told me that McKinley was cold and high and dangerous, so I was not unaware of the difficulties. Over the years, many people have asked me how I trained for such a major climb. I tell them I didn't train. I didn't exercise and I didn't run. I pushed a baby carriage. That's how I got in shape for Mount McKinley.

I was a wife and a mother and I had my family duties. The general thinking at the time was that a woman's place was in the home, and some people were appalled that I would pick up and go to Alaska for three months. But I found later, after I got home and after all the attention that was showered on me for making the climb, that other women mostly admired what I had done. They wanted to know how I did it.

I never felt that I should be seen as any kind of hero. I felt I was the one who was lucky enough to get to go to this spectacular place. The fact is that I was fortunate to have a husband who always wanted me to share his travels. Doors closed to other women were opened for me this way. Climbing Mount McKinley was not the last great adventure of my life. In fact, my life has been filled with great adventures all over the world.

Chapter *One*

THE EDUCATION OF A YOUNG GIRL

THERE WAS LITTLE IN MY CHILDHOOD that foreshadowed the outdoors life I was destined to lead, though my father did take me on Sunday afternoon walks into the woods about a mile from our home in West Roxbury, Massachusetts, a community just outside Boston. I remember climbing on big rocks that were called Roxbury puddingstone and being told that the small rocks in the big rocks were like raisins in a pudding. I would climb to the top of these big boulders and shout "I'm king of the castle!"

Looking back, it is clear that I always loved excitement. By the time I was ten, my great treat was to be put on a train alone to go visit my grandparents. It seemed like such a long journey, from West Roxbury to West Medway. It was only about a one-hour ride, but it seemed as if I were on my way to Alaska.

Somehow the adventurous spirit was in my blood. Even as a youngster, I preferred the company of boys. They wanted to do riskier things than girls did, so they were more stimulating to be around. I assumed that any boy I met would lead me into adventure.

◀ I was about three years old in 1918 when this picture was taken at my home near Boston. Next to me is my brother, Alvar Jr.; then my mother, Maybell; my father, Alvar W. Polk; and my sister, Edith.

When I was growing up in the 1920s and 1930s, it was a very different time in this country. A girl was expected to behave in certain ways. I was brought up to be an asset to my husband, to be a good mother, and to be an active volunteer in the community. When I asked Irwin Griswold, a family friend who was dean of Harvard Law School, why I couldn't attend the school, which had no women students, his reasoning was: "You would get married, have babies, and take the place of a man who has to make a living."

That was the thinking back then.

I was born Barbara Polk, on November 10, 1914, and my father, Alvar, climbed out onto the porch on the second story of our home and hoisted the Stars and Stripes. It was a signal to the neighborhood that a baby girl had been born. He was joyful to have a daughter because he already had two sons—my brother Alvar Jr., a year and a half older than I, and another boy, Hadley, by a previous marriage.

I weighed six and a half pounds and had a dimple in each cheek. My mother, Maybell, wrote in my baby book: "She was the happiest, sweetest baby that ever lived. She rarely cried, but had a forceful temper which relieved its fury by bumps on the floor with her forehead."

My mother had been adopted. Her natural parents were from Scotland, but they died by the time she was twelve and she was raised in Boston by her adoptive family. My father was born in Ohio, one of eleven children of a Universalist minister and his wife.

Two of my father's sisters set fine examples for me of active womanhood. My favorite aunt, Cora Polk Dewick, was the first female graduate of Tufts University. And my aunt Mary Polk was head of the French department in the Boston schools.

I apparently did not cause my parents much trouble until I came down with bronchial pneumonia at age four and nearly died. At the same time—with my new baby sister, Edith, only three weeks old—my father had septic pneumonia. There were no antibiotics in those days, and my mother said it was a terrible siege for us all.

My passage through the childhood diseases of chicken pox, whooping cough, and stomach upsets was not unusual, although I did have scarlet fever and measles at the same time. A red poster on the front door announced that our household was quarantined. Looking out my bedroom window I could see what I thought were ten-foot snowdrifts, and I envied the kids coasting on the hill. The family doctor came to see me every day and put pennies at the foot of my bed, encouraging me to muster the strength to crawl to them. After I recovered, I became healthy and strong. In high school and college, I seldom missed a day of classes, and I developed great stamina in adulthood.

Several childhood incidents stick clearly in my mind, mostly pleasant ones. There were gas lights on our street, and every evening the lamplighter came to our neighborhood carrying a long pole. He walked up the street inserting this pole into each lamp, making it burst into a small flame that lit the surrounding area. I thought this was miraculous. I ran down the street to meet him each evening, then continued along with him, chatting all the way while he lit the lamps.

Another happy memory is of the adventure called "pung hopping." After a snowstorm, the milkman made his deliveries in a box-shaped sleigh known as a pung. He rang a tinkling bell as he passed through the neighborhood, and the kids rushed out of their houses and hopped on the runners of the sleigh. He let us ride, screaming and giggling, while he made his rounds.

I wasn't naughty very often, but occasionally I bent the rules. I played hooky one day when a friend suggested we go to the woods and pick flowers. We had an exciting adventure in the fairyland forest, but when I saw the expression on my mother's face, I knew I was in trouble. I told her I had gone to the woods instead of to school, and she spanked me with a small hairbrush.

I once made a halfhearted attempt to run away from home after I had been sent to my room for some transgression. I wanted to get even with my parents and I knew there could be no worse punishment for them

With a mirror and a powder puff, I made last-minute preparations for performing during a ballet evening at Boston's West Roxbury Women's Club when I was about ten years old.

than to find their child gone. I climbed out the window of my room onto a slanting porch, then jumped to the ground and hid in the bushes. The dilemma was how long to hide before they began panicking and started looking for me. After a short time in the bushes, I returned, sheepishly, and nothing more was said. They were just relieved to see me.

When I was about eight, I was given aesthetic dance lessons and made to perform on occasions such as the May festival. For my butterfly dance, my mother made a lovely costume with accordion-pleated wings of apricot chiffon, and antennae in a crown of wire pinned into my hair. A butterfly dance didn't amount to doing much of anything—it mostly meant you tried to be graceful.

I didn't really enjoy being forced to perform, and by the age of about ten, my aesthetic dance career was over. Instead I began piano lessons. My mother insisted I practice a half hour every day. The older I got, the more tedious piano-playing seemed, and occasionally I moved the big hand of the living room clock forward a few minutes so I could escape early to play with my friends.

I continued piano lessons until I left for college, even though I was more interested in boys than music by then. My final recital took place in my teacher's home. Wearing a new dress, I played a piece called "Juba," putting heart and soul into the lively number. "Rustles of Spring" didn't go as well. My fingers were rolling nimbly up and down the piano, but I kept returning to the beginning and panicking because I couldn't find the final chord. When I finally found it, I concluded the piece with a flourish.

Of course none of this dancing or piano playing prepared me for being a mountain climber. It was just part of the well-rounded education of a young woman in those days. Nobody offered young ladies instruction in putting on crampons or wielding ice axes.

Chapter Two

A Year in France

I attended Boston Girls Latin School when it gave the best classical education in the country. It was not, however, the best school for offering sports teams. Back then Girls Latin had a field hockey team. That's all. There were not many choices if you were an athletically inclined girl. But in any case, rather than play sports, I preferred to go to the library and meet a certain boy.

At the age of sixteen, I entered Smith College, in Northampton, Massachusetts. I was an especially young freshman because I had skipped the fifth grade. And I looked young for my age. I was small—five-foot-one and 115 pounds—blond and blue-eyed, and I had those dimples. I was also quite naive in my knowledge of the world. I will say that my family was ahead of its time in some ways, because they always assumed I would go to college.

Preparing for college was so much easier back then. Kids today have to impress admissions directors with their extracurricular activities. I don't recall having to write an essay about my life or why I wanted to go to Smith. All I had to do was pass the College Board exams.

It was a very hot day in June when I took the exams, and the room was not air-conditioned. I got a high mark in chemistry but failed geometry. The school allowed me to be tutored in that subject and I was admitted.

Many of us reported a week early to take a course called freshman hygiene. We learned how babies were made, which came as a shock to many of us. Nowadays children in kindergarten know more than we did then.

My roommate was much more sophisticated than I was. When she signed out to go away for the weekend, she asked me to tell our housemother that she was visiting her grandmother. I knew it wasn't the grandmother she was spending the weekend with. But I wasn't asked, so I didn't have to lie.

Soon enough I changed rooms and developed a close friendship with my new roommate, Frances Gelabert—a friendship that has lasted more than sixty years. Frances was an attractive girl with large brown eyes, high cheekbones, pink cheeks, and an outgoing personality. She was from Tulsa, Oklahoma, and won a scholarship to Smith by writing a composition on fertilizer. We giggled our way through college, and we still talk about how we supported each other when things got tough.

Academically I did reasonably well. For my freshman biology final exam, the professor placed a split lobster in front of me and asked me to describe its reproductive system. I nervously plunged ahead until the professor stopped me to say, "That's fine, Miss Polk, but you have described a female reproductive system and this happens to be a male lobster." Undaunted, I immediately launched into a description of the male reproductive system. I passed the test.

One day, as a form of hazing, I was called upon at lunch to lead the residents of my house in singing the Smith College song. In spite of my fear I stood up and led the group, swinging my arms like an orchestra conductor. To my amazement I was chosen to advance in the competition for a song leader for the college. I had to perform before the entire student body at chapel service—an experience so frightening that I have only a vague recollection of it. It was not the kind of fright you find in climbing mountains; it was absolutely more scary.

I applied to take my junior year abroad, though my family couldn't afford it, and I was accepted. I received a partial scholarship and an uncle helped pay for the rest. Thirty-two of us left New York in August 1933, adorned in white gloves and hats. We were a bit nervous. Most of us had never been to Europe, and traveling by boat for ten days before landing at Le Havre reminded us of how far from home we would be. An older couple who shared a dining table on the ship with Fran and me ordered a bottle of champagne, and we got quite tipsy. That was my first drink.

Our first eight weeks were spent at the University of Grenoble, immersed in French language classes. We may have written papers on French literature, but most of us couldn't order a ham sandwich in French. During an oral exam in front of an audience that included Fran and the French family that we were staying with—a widow and her adult daughter—the professor asked me to explain in French how to make bread. This was a problem because I didn't have any idea how to make bread, in French *or* English. I pulled several French words out of my mind that pertained to bread making, though I didn't have the faintest idea what to do with the ingredients. But when I sat down, the professor said I had done very well: "*Vous avez bien-fait. Merci, Mademoiselle.*"

Just before Christmas, we moved to Paris to attend the Sorbonne. On the train from Grenoble to Paris, I had my first glimpse of dramatic tall mountains. As we wound through the Alps, I shrieked to my friends, "Look at those peaks! They're so high!" Little could I imagine that a few years later I would be standing atop mountains even higher. The Alps made a big impression on me. Until then the largest mountain I had ever seen was Mount Washington in New Hampshire, not much more than 6,000 feet high.

In Paris, once again my French family consisted of an elderly lady with an unmarried daughter, who was secretary to a physicist at the Sorbonne. The professor was invited to dinner one night, and I stunned everyone at the end of the meal by declaring, "*Que je suis pleine!*" I thought I was telling them how full I was. It was explained to me that the proper expression was "*Que j'ai bien mangé!*" I had announced that I was pregnant.

We had to have chaperones if we went out in the evening, and we were required to be home for dinner by eight. We laughed about this rule because we could get into plenty of mischief before then. We spent many afternoons after class in cafes on the Boulevard Montparnasse or tea dancing at Club Raspail. We discovered that a little wine before going home made our French much more fluent, but I don't think we fooled our French family for a minute. Madame knew what we were up to, and she was also aware how French boys were lying in wait for the famous Smith College students. American girls had a reputation.

Brian Hetherington, a friend of mine who lived in England, invited me to visit his home. My parents had to send a letter from the United States before I was allowed to go. This was another exciting adventure. I sailed across the English Channel and took a train to Hampstead, where Brian's mother fed me a high tea and looked me over carefully to make sure I wasn't one of those "loose" American girls. On Christmas Eve we attended the village church service, and on Christmas morning I was awakened by the sound of bugles. I rushed into the yard and saw hunters in red jackets and black velvet caps galloping across the fields, on a fox hunt. On New Year's Eve, Brian and I attended a dance at the town hall. Then it was time to take the boat train back to Paris and school.

Our Sorbonne education differed greatly from life at Smith. We had large lecture classes and almost no contact with professors. Except for our one main supervisor, Professor Guilloton, we were on our own. He kept us on track, assigned homework, gave us exams, and ran class discussions.

When I was overseas I had my first sobering experience with international politics. Fran and I saw an ad on a bulletin board about a free trip to Germany over Easter vacation in 1934. We were invited for a two-week visit to Cologne to live with a German family. It turned out to be part of a program to indoctrinate foreigners in the policies of Adolf Hitler.

The experiment backfired somewhat on the Nazis, as far as we were concerned. The couple we stayed with were so saddened by what they saw happening in their country that they didn't try to propagandize us. But still their young son greeted us at breakfast each morning wearing a Hitler Youth uniform and proudly brandishing a small sword bearing the words *Blut und Ruhm* (Blood and Glory).

Fran and I knew nothing about Hitler, and at first we did not take him or the Nazis seriously. We were severely scolded by the conductor of a trolley car for making fun of the "Heil Hitler" salute. He told us he would throw us off the car if we did it again.

Older members of the Nazi youth movement were assigned to entertain our group of eight foreign students, and we spent evenings in bistros dancing, drinking Rhine wine, and having heated arguments about Hitler's ideas. If a Nazi wanted to cut in on your dancing partner, he would do his "Heil Hitler" salute and click his heels together. This ridiculous performance always made me giggle. But I soon learned there was nothing funny about what these young men were doing or thinking and that they didn't tolerate being made fun of.

One member of our group was a Jewish student from Dartmouth College. When he was insulted by a German student, Fran and I rose to his defense, and it became clear to us that Hitler was dead serious about persecuting the Jews. Another time, one of the Nazis began to describe Hitler's plans for invading the Netherlands. I was indignant. "We would never let you do it!" I said.

I was very disturbed by what I saw happening in Germany, and when I returned to the United States I wrote an article on the subject for *The Christian Leader*, a magazine published by the Universalist Church. Back at Smith College I had heated arguments with my German language professor, who tried to sell us on the glories of Hitler.

My senior year at Smith was not as eventful as my junior year in Europe, but I had a run-in with good old Professor Guilloton, formerly of the Sorbonne and now head of our French department. I worked very hard on a difficult French translation assignment and he gave me a grade of A. But he also wrote, "You must have cheated." I was furious and wrote him a letter telling him that he was wrong. When I told my date that evening about the incident, he suggested a little revenge on the professor. Let the air out of his car tires, he said. We did it.

My graduation ceremonies were thrilling because Anne Lindbergh received an honorary degree, and present was Charles Lindbergh himself, the greatest American hero of his time for his solo flight across the Atlantic. I had always envied Anne Lindbergh's life of adventure.

The summer after graduation I worked at Dennison House, a settlement house near Chinatown in Boston. I taught arts and crafts to young girls and played volleyball with them on the street after supper. My piano playing came in handy when the boys' instructor suggested we produce a musical.

At that time a woman's choices were narrow. For the most part, we could either marry or become teachers. I had an offer to go to the IBM training school, but I couldn't attend the interview so I didn't get in. Luckily. Otherwise I never would have met Bradford Washburn.

At Dennison House I lived in the room that Amelia Earhart occupied when she was a social worker there. I knew the public facts—about how she was a famous flyer and was lost trying to cross the Pacific. What I did not know at the time was that my future husband, Brad, had been interviewed to be the navigator on that ill-fated flight.

Brad had suggested to Earhart that her plane should have a trailing antenna so she could pick up a radio signal on Howland Island. He knew how difficult it would be to locate this tiny island and that she could easily miss it and run out of gas over the ocean. When she told Brad she didn't want to take the time to install radio equipment on Howland Island, Brad told her he wasn't interested in being the navigator. I have always believed that her flight might have been successful if she had taken his advice.

After my summer job with the children, I decided I didn't really care to be a teacher. I wanted to get into a more exciting part of the academic world, at a college, and the best way then for a woman to gain entrance to a place like that was to become a secretary. So in 1936 I went to Pierce Secretarial School. Then I landed a job that seemed to have interesting potential. I became secretary to several professors in the biology department at Harvard.

I enjoyed my job, and my boss even allowed me to take three weeks off without pay to go to Europe. I was twenty-three by then, and I knew I could never settle down until I got Europe out of my system. I returned to France and enjoyed a nostalgic visit to the Sorbonne, looking up old friends. World War II was coming, but it had not yet touched France. Then I went back to my Harvard job and settled in.

CHAPTER 3

LOVE AND MARRIAGE

IN THE COURSE OF ONE'S LIFE, fate has a way of intervening. My professors were keeping me busy and things were going fine, but one day in 1939 the mailman asked me a question that decided my future. Clarkie asked me if I would interview for a job with a man named Bradford Washburn, who had just become director of the New England Museum of Natural History. Clarkie said Washburn was desperate to find a qualified secretary and had asked him to keep an eye out for someone as he delivered the mail.

I had read in the newspaper about a famous young explorer and mountain climber becoming director of the museum, but I hadn't seen a picture of him. My initial reply to Clarkie was a firm "No." I said, "I don't want to work in an old museum and I definitely don't want to work for a crazy mountain climber!"

Clarkie didn't give up. Every day when he delivered our mail he brought it up again, saying, "Give it a try." Finally I gave in and made an appointment for an interview, even though I had no intention of leaving my job.

Late one afternoon, a biology graduate student I was dating drove me across town to the museum for an interview. I expected to stay for such a

◀ Brad and I were married April 27, 1940, in the Harvard University Chapel. I had little inkling then of the extraordinary adventures that lay ahead.

short time that I asked him to keep the car double parked. "I will make short shrift of this guy," I said. "I don't want to work in this dreary place."

My heart sank as I entered the museum. It seemed even more depressing than I remembered. As a child my parents took me there quite often, and I had a vivid recollection of the whale skeleton hanging from the ceiling. It was still there, covered with layers of dust. All of the other exhibits seemed equally dreary and I wondered why an explorer would want to work in such a dingy place.

I found my way to the library for our meeting. The room was undergoing construction, so I sat down on a long board balanced between two chairs and waited nervously for Bradford Washburn. I didn't know what to expect and I didn't know what a modern explorer would look like. When he emerged from behind the book stacks, I was very surprised. He was rather slight, had no beard, and bore no resemblance to the pictures of explorers I had seen in history books, pictures of men like Lewis and Clark. Brad was a youngster, about to turn twenty-nine at the time.

He immediately joined me on the long board and began to describe in detail the requirements for becoming his secretary. I listened politely, but when he began talking about handling museum finances, I said quickly, "I don't know anything about finances."

"But you can learn, can't you?" he replied.

After a respectable amount of time, I said I had another appointment and had to leave. He urged me to think about the opportunity and said he would call me in two weeks.

I still had no intention of taking the job, but one thing I had overlooked in Brad was his determination and persistence. Rather than waiting two weeks, he called me every day for two weeks to make sure I was really thinking it over. Brad was not being coy or flirtatious. He was very businesslike, but he kept calling.

One day, talking the situation over with my father, it came to me that perhaps this was a good opportunity. I said, "If this man is so determined and persuasive, I'm inclined to think this museum will go places. Maybe I'd be smart to take this job."

I started working as Bradford Washburn's secretary on March 28, 1939. The job was stressful. He stood behind me while I typed a report for the museum trustees. Everything had to be done in a hurry, and there always seemed to be a crisis.

After initially feeling overwhelmed by the job, it started to become fascinating. I did learn about finances. The auditor who came to examine the museum accounts taught me how to balance a checkbook. He teased me about my plodding but conscientious technique, then taught me a better way.

The museum had a public lecture series and I enjoyed meeting the speakers. Something exciting was always happening. One day Captain Bob Bartlett, who had been on a North Pole expedition with Admiral Perry, surprised me in the office by shouting, "Where the hell is Bradford Washburn?" Captain Bob was a colorful person and every other word was a swear word, but meeting characters like Bartlett spiced up my work.

My relationship with the boss was very formal. He was demanding, but as long as I gave him good work, he was never cross with me. I even got up the courage to ask for a vacation to visit my brother in Galveston, Texas, after working there for only three months. Much to my surprise, he granted me permission to take off for two weeks. He was inquisitive and interested about the details when I returned.

A few weeks later, as I was concentrating on balancing the museum's checking account, the office door suddenly opened and Brad asked, "Would you like to go flying?" I was surprised by the invitation, but I accepted. We drove to the small airport in East Boston and I climbed into the seat beside him, trembling with a combination of excitement and fear. There was a practical reason for the flight, Brad explained to me. In order to keep his license he had to fly a certain number of hours a month, but his new job made it difficult to find the time. This was not a date.

I changed the subject and asked what would happen if he pushed the stick forward. The next thing I knew, the small plane went into a dive. I grabbed whatever was nearest me and almost stopped breathing as Brad said, "That's what happens!" That was the last question I asked.

On another occasion, during the winter, Brad invited me to go flying after work. This time it was in an open cockpit plane and I had to put on a flying suit, helmet, and goggles and climb into the back cockpit. We flew over Boston and landed at the Navy Air Base in Squantum. I can still remember how excited I felt. I imagined I was Anne Lindbergh flying off to the Orient.

Just before Christmas, Brad called me into his office and asked if I would help him write his holiday cards. He had a very long list of friends and business associates. After a lengthy session of addressing, he invited me to dinner. He took me to Hayes Bickford's in Harvard Square, a less-than-elegant cafeteria. And then he let me go home on the subway!

One weekend in January 1940, Brad was in Hartford, Connecticut, to give a lecture at the Travelers Insurance Company. He was a popular lecturer on mountaineering and supported his Alaska expeditions by photography, lecturing, and writing. That same weekend I was scheduled to visit New York to see a friend who was in the Navy. Mac, a museum employee who was driving to Hartford to handle the photo projector for Brad's lecture, invited me to drive that far with him. I'd take the train the rest of the way. When we got to Hartford, I discovered there wasn't another train to New York for hours, and I would have to make the rest of my trip on the night train. Mac suggested I go to Brad's lecture in the meanwhile.

Brad showed beautiful pictures and I thoroughly enjoyed the lecture. When the lights went up, he saw me and rushed over, asking, "What in the world are you doing here?"

When I told him I was going to New York for a weekend date, he told me that he was also heading for New York that night. He asked if I had a berth on the train. When I said I did not, he offered me his and said he would get another. The other one turned out to be the berth above mine. This made me nervous. I wasn't sure it was appropriate for a secretary to be seen with her boss outside the office.

But there was no impropriety involved, and since we were so exhausted we just crawled into our berths. Suddenly I saw an arm moving down the wall from the berth above, with the hand obviously trying to signal "Good night." I was in a quandary. If I squeezed his hand, he might think I was too aggressive. If I didn't, he might get angry. So I let instinct guide me. I squeezed Brad's hand gently and whispered "Good night."

In the morning, Brad asked that I join him and the radio personality Lowell Thomas for breakfast at a New York hotel. I said, "Oh, no, Lowell Thomas wouldn't want to have breakfast with me!"

Brad insisted. He said that I had typed so many of his letters to Lowell Thomas that of course he would be delighted to meet me. I acquiesced. Much later, Lowell told me he had informed his wife that evening that Brad and I were getting married. He said he had seen it in our eyes, even though neither Brad nor I had yet expressed any particular feelings for one another.

After breakfast we went our separate ways. I met my date, and after a pleasant two days, he escorted me to Penn Station to take the four o'clock train back to Boston. Imagine my surprise when Brad turned up on the station platform! My date told us many years later that he knew his goose was cooked when he saw that Brad was taking the same train.

It was a five-hour ride, and out of the office we both became more relaxed human beings. I began to feel some tinglings of desire from Brad, and something inside me was responding. I could hardly wait to get to work the next morning, and when Brad arrived at the office, I could feel myself blushing.

Brad is not a person to shilly-shally. When he wants something badly, he goes after it. He gave me a ride home the following evening, and I invited him in. As we were sitting on a sofa in my living room, he suddenly asked if I loved him enough to marry him.

I surprised myself by replying that I did. I sometimes wonder why I didn't question him then about what kind of life he expected me to lead. But I didn't ask, and he didn't bring up the subject. He must have already gotten a glimpse of my sense of adventure.

Our engagement was so sudden that the museum staff was electrified when Brad announced the news at a small tea in the library. I immediately resigned my job. In those days that was the proper thing to do.

We were married two months later, on April 27, 1940. The marriage took place in the Harvard University Chapel, with close friends and relatives as bridesmaids and ushers and about two hundred people attending. The reception followed at the Harvard Faculty Club.

I never could have expected the adventures I was to experience throughout my married life—and they began right at the wedding. One of our ushers put a padlock on the sleeve of the jacket Brad was to wear, and there was no way Brad could get into the jacket. I knew nothing about the crisis. Brad ran to the nearest hardware store for a file to remove the lock and he was totally out of breath by the time he got back for the ceremony. As he stood beside me taking the wedding vows, his voice was so weak that I thought perhaps he had lost his courage about going through with it. And after the ceremony, one of the other ushers hid my going-away clothes. I quickly came to the conclusion that Brad's mountain climbing friends were a strange lot.

We spent our honeymoon in a ski cabin Brad had built in New Hampshire, on eleven acres he had purchased from Mr. Gile, the local gas station operator, for a thousand dollars. Brad called this cabin his dowry. It was on top of a hill with a magnificent view of Mount Washington. The cabin stood two hundred yards from the main road, with only a steep footpath leading from the road to the door.

This seemed like a wonderful place for a honeymoon, but on the way Brad suddenly realized the cabin didn't have appropriate bedroom furniture. His mountaineering and ski friends had probably been sleeping on air mattresses. As we drove to the cabin, we saw a sign in a store window in the town of Conway advertising a bedroom furniture sale. We stopped and bought a double bed, mattress and spring, and two chests of drawers. We arranged to have the bed delivered later that day at Mr. Gile's "last chance" gas station, but it was our responsibility to haul it up the hill.

We arrived at the cabin late in the afternoon, had a quick meal, and then began to figure out how to get the bed up the hill. Brad found a packboard that had been used on his expeditions, and we hiked back down the hill. Sure enough the bed had been delivered and was sitting in Mr. Giles' yard. It was very dark by the time we started tying bed parts onto the packboard. It took us several trips up and down the hill. I led with a lantern while Brad did the carrying. The last thing up was the bedspring. This was quite challenging. The spring was bouncy and Brad kept losing his footing.

We saw Mr. Giles the next morning, and apparently he had been watching us from his bedroom window. He had a toothless smile and a thick New England accent, and on this day he had a twinkle in his eye when he said, "It don't take you young folks long to get into a double bed, does it?"

We spent two wonderful weeks at the cabin, hiking and skiing. When we returned to our small apartment in Boston to start our married life, we were shocked to see the news. Hitler had invaded the Netherlands. I screamed, "That's just what those Nazi boys in Germany said they were going to do!"

It took me some time to adjust to being a housewife with no job to go to every day. I soon discovered, though, that there were many responsibilities in being a museum director's wife. One event I shall never forget was my first dinner party, before a lecture by the Greenland explorer Admiral Donald MacMillan. My mother had tried in vain to teach me to cook, but somehow I prepared a respectable meal of roast chicken, rice, and vegetables for Admiral MacMillan and the museum trustees.

Trying to make a fancy dessert was my downfall. My meringues-glaces looked delicious with ice cream and chocolate sauce on top, but when we began to eat them, all conversation stopped. I had not baked the meringues long enough, and they were so chewy our mouths were near paralyzed. It was obviously a memorable experience: Fifty years later one of the trustees reminded me about my meringues, and we had a long laugh.

It was only about a month after our marriage that Brad and I were deep into the planning of my first Alaska expedition, an attempt to make the first ascent of Mount Bertha in Alaska's Fairweather Range.

CHAPTER 4

Four

NORTH TO ALASKA

IN THE TIME LEADING UP TO OUR WEDDING, Brad never mentioned a thing about his mountain climbing in Alaska. He never suggested any plans for long expeditions, and he definitely never said he would like me to climb with him. I had no mountaineering background. The extent of my experience was climbing a 4,000-foot mountain with a date, right after college. That wasn't the best day of my life. It was hard work and I was out of breath the whole time.

Shortly after Brad and I were married I heard him talking on the phone about an expedition to Southeastern Alaska. For several years he had been leading mountain trips to Alaska during the summer, and his photographs and lectures provided income to fund more adventures. It became obvious that Brad expected me to join him on this latest trip. I soon found myself testing dehydrated food in my kitchen. The neighbors began complaining about terrible odors coming through the vents into their apartments. When we explained what we were doing—testing food for an expedition—they became remarkably compliant.

I knew absolutely nothing about Alaska. It was still a frontier, and just the thought of it was thrilling. The object of the journey for the summer of 1940 was Mount Bertha, a 10,182-foot mountain near Glacier Bay, in the Fairweather Range, that had never been climbed. I had no real feeling about being a pioneering woman on a serious Alaskan expedition. I only knew that as the only woman, I had to measure up.

We invited four Harvard students to go with us: Tom Winship, then captain of the Harvard ski team (and later editor of the *Boston Globe*), Alva Morrison, Maynard Miller, and Lee Wilson—all of them not yet twenty years old. A few weeks before we were scheduled to leave, Lowell Thomas asked Brad to take his sixteen-year-old son along. The son was in boarding school and Lowell felt that he could use an exciting adventure. So this was how I got to know Lowell Thomas Jr., who later became lieutenant governor of Alaska and a famous bush pilot.

Brad had a good reputation for bringing his expedition members home safely, but I always felt Lowell figured this trip wouldn't be too tough because Brad was bringing me along. Lowell also talked us into taking Michl Feuersinger, an Austrian ski instructor who was in his mid-twenties. Secretly I thought he might teach me to ski better.

Brad wanted to use sled dogs on this trip because we would have a long trek to Mount Bertha across Brady Glacier from Hugh Miller Inlet after leaving our boat. We borrowed six dogs from a good friend, Norman Vaughan, and Bill Shearer. Norman had traveled to Antarctica with Admiral Byrd in 1928, and later became known in Alaska for competing in the Iditarod Trail Sled Dog Race. Remarkably, at the age of eighty-nine he returned to Antarctica and climbed the 10,000-foot mountain that had been named for him decades earlier.

We left Boston on June 20, 1940. Preparations were hectic up to the last minute. The dogs arrived late, so Brad barely made the farewell dinner party given by our parents. Some of the museum staff came to the train station to see us off, and we departed for Montreal amidst shouts of "Farewell," the flashing of cameras, and the barking of dogs. The dogs were staked out in the baggage car. By the time we tumbled into our berths, we were exhausted.

Once in Canada, we had to switch trains—a huge organizational project. The dogs were taken out at the station. Then we had to catch the Continental Limited, which left from another station. No taxi driver wanted to take us with all our bags, the dogs, and gear. We finally found a ride. The conductor was already shouting "All aboard!" when Brad, Lee, and I came rushing up. The dogs were in a frenzy. We pushed them into the baggage car and Brad tied them up so they wouldn't fight.

By the time we found all of our baggage and an empty berth and had moved in, we had caused quite a sensation. The other passengers were irritated by the commotion, but when we explained our expedition, they became intrigued and tried to help us. The train trip west across Canada to Prince Rupert, British Columbia, took five days—with something wild happening just about every day.

The first night, I got lost in the dark and started to climb into bed with a strange man. On the second night, the porter shook Brad awake to tell him the dogs were fighting. We raced to the baggage car in our pajamas and were flabbergasted at the sight that greeted us. Huge cartons of tissues had been stored at one end of the car, and the dogs had gotten into them. Nikko had pulled himself loose from the chain and bitten Jeddo very badly on the nose, then tore up the Kleenex. The car was filled with bloody Kleenex. Brad grabbed an empty pail and plowed into the fighting dogs, hitting them on the nose to make them stop, while I cowered in the corner.

A newspaper reporter turned up at the station in Winnipeg and took pictures of us. While I was still outside at the station, the train started to get under way. Brad yanked me into the baggage car just in time. Eventually our ride became more peaceful. We were able to enjoy the scenery, although we all caught colds. In British Columbia we were especially struck by the beauty of 12,000-foot Mount Robson.

We made the transfer to the S.S. *Prince George*, bound for Alaska. I was treated to my first view of glaciers, and the spectacular scenery had me in a state of ecstasy. Late in the evening we stopped at Ketchikan, Alaska, a town built on pilings above the water, with board sidewalks and streets. The boat also stopped at small villages to take on Natives who later disembarked at other places that had canneries. We anchored in front of the Taku Glacier to offload cargo for the Polaris Mine. The two-hundred-foot-high ice towers at the face of the glacier gleamed a gorgeous turquoise-blue.

We reached Juneau on June 27, and our first priority was to find a place for the dogs. A friend came to the rescue, offering us the use of a barn. Brad did not feel well, and we stayed an extra day in Juneau. The delay gave us the opportunity to have lunch at the home of Alaska Governor Ernest Gruening. Another guest, an attractive, large man, turned out to be the opera star Lauritz Melchior. We didn't recognize his name and thought he was a wealthy Danish baron, in Alaska to hunt bears. Later we read in the society column of the local paper that Mr. and Mrs. Washburn had dined with the famous opera singer.

Two days after arriving in Juneau, we boarded the fishing boat *Forester*, piloted by Ginky Bayers, and headed for Glacier Bay and Hugh Miller Inlet. Some of us slept on deck and others slept in bunks, but we rose early to watch as we sailed into the inlet. We unloaded and the boat took off, leaving us alone. Suddenly I realized there was no turning back. It was now just me and the boys, and I had to keep up.

Our group packed loads up the hill from the shore of the inlet to our base camp site all afternoon. I carried a few small loads, but spent most of the time unpacking food. For supper we fried salmon that we had picked up at a cannery along the way. We set up three tents at base camp, and Brad and I were in the "bridal suite." It was almost 10:00 p.m. by the time we finished establishing base camp, but it was still very light out, with magnificent sun and shadows. Our camp looked just like Little America, Admiral Byrd's camp in Antarctica.

July 1 was Tom Winship's birthday. Alva, Michl, and Maynard moved on up to our next camp site, but the rest of us at base camp celebrated for

Win with twenty candles stuck on a piece of wood. This was my first day of camping and I enjoyed it. We fooled around getting breakfast. I cooked eggs, but Lowell picked up the collapsible frying pan and upset half of them. All we could do was laugh.

We radioed to Juneau and asked for a plane to come out and carry some of our supplies to higher elevations. The pilot, Alex Holden, was hampered by cloudy weather, and circled three times without ever seeing us. It was disheartening. When we radioed again to Juneau, they asked why we hadn't built a fire to make it easier for Alex to see us.

I took my first steps on a glacier the next day. And I jumped over my first crevasse. I knew it could be dangerous, but it wasn't half bad. For the trek to Camp 2, some of us made the mistake of wearing our regular boots instead of climbing boots and had a dreadful time slipping on the ice. Maynard and Lee wore climbing boots, so they chopped steps for us. It took us about three hours to make four miles.

Lee had a tough day. He had forgotten to tie up the wind-powered battery charger the night before, and when a southeaster kicked up, the propeller broke. That meant our battery could not be charged, and hence no radio. Then Brad gave Lee the minimum thermometer, which he proceeded to break.

Independence Day was different from any other Fourth of July I ever spent. Brad woke us up with two shots of a pistol in honor of the holiday.

The next night we had a terrible scare. We let the dogs go free for a few minutes, and in no time fights were raging. Brad hit Nikko with a pail. The dogs were a lot nicer the next day, and they took me on a rocky ride on the sled. Wolf tried to play it coy, and Jeddo didn't understand a word I yelled at him. The boys told me I wouldn't have much luck driving a dog team unless I learned to swear, because that was the language the dogs were accustomed to. But I was brought up in a family where swearing was not permitted. I actually tried a few mild swear words to get the dogs going, but fortunately "mush," "gee," and "haw" produced the necessary response most of the time.

Young and exuberant, the members of our team were ready for the attempt on Mount Bertha. In the back row, from left to right, are Lee Wilson, Alva Morrison, Michl Feuersinger, and Lowell Thomas Jr. In the front row are Maynard Miller, Bradford Washburn, Barbara Washburn, and Tom Winship.

Pilot Alex Holden finally flew in with his floatplane, and we packed it full of supplies and gear to be airdropped higher up the route. We flew up Brady Glacier and spotted the rest of our party. From the plane, we threw out thirty-three bundles in forty-five minutes—a total of 1,500 pounds. I had never seen such country: rugged snowcapped peaks everywhere, with glaciers and inlets tucked between them. Mount Bertha and Mount Crillon were in clouds, but what we were able to see was magnificent.

A day later we all moved up to Camp 2 to stay, driving the dogs. It took two hours to get them across the huge glacier. We mushed along the left side of the sled, Brad riding and pushing it, Alva pulling, and me coming along behind. Brad pulled off a spectacular stunt. The sled knocked him into a crevasse, but with the help of centrifugal force he ran up the other side of it and jumped out!

The whole climbing process involved moving up the mountain stage by stage, camp by camp. When we left for Camp 3 to ferry supplies, Brad and I drove the dogs. Jeddo didn't understand signals at all and I had to lead him all the way. It was tough going up the steep pitches. I thought my legs would cave in. I carried my belongings tied securely to a packboard. I was able to carry forty pounds without too much agony, but at low altitude the boys were carrying up to a hundred pounds each.

When we finally moved to Camp 3 to stay, it began raining steadily. Michl found some delicious water in the rocks nearby, so we didn't have to melt snow anymore. But we couldn't find the sugar or the cereal. They may have been lost being dumped from the plane.

We made the move up from Camp 3 on a day that was hotter than Hades and wretchedly bright on the flat glacier. My face got burned to a crisp. Maynard, Lee, and Alva put up two tents, then left me alone while they returned to Camp 3. I was in a magnificent spot. You could see the sea in the distance.

On July 17, more than two weeks after leaving the boat, we finally made camp right under Mount Bertha. The dogs traveled the six miles to the camp fairly well, although I had to keep my eye on Jeddo most of the way. The snow was slushy and we got into a bit of fog but managed to follow the trail established the night before by three of our climbers. As we traveled, the crest of Mount La Perouse emerged, bathed in pink. Summits showing above the fog created an eerie effect.

A couple of days later the boys took a look over the hill near camp and then reported some shocking news. A huge icefall choked the route to the pass we had intended to reach. We decided to establish a new camp, farther to the right at the end of a ridge. It was a route that had been rejected earlier in favor of the pass.

Our move was followed by a series of rainy days. We did have some excitement, though. Brad set a can of gasoline down inside a tent, but the cap was not on tight. A stream of gas trickled toward the burning Primus stove and caught fire, sending flames leaping up under our feet. We began

We made base camp on the Brady Glacier. Our climbing route took us up the east spur of Mount Bertha.

throwing things and stamping on the flames, which didn't do any good. Brad opened the tent door in a hurry, I leaped out, and Lee tossed the gas can out after me. It was a close shave.

July 26 was a clear day, so we decided to start up Bertha. It was taking so long that morning to melt water that, instead, we used the dishwater from the night before to make our oatmeal. It was not good. Poor Michl couldn't even swallow it.

We didn't begin climbing until 11:30, and we got under way without a specific destination—just seeing how far we could get. Brad chopped steps and we had a fixed rope, so the going wasn't too bad. I was on a rope with Brad, and he stopped to take pictures so often that I got chances to rest. There were some tough spots for me, though, including the move over a knife-edged cornice. My ice axe technique was not perfect, so I took a short slide into a pile of rocks and skinned my elbow.

When we stopped for lunch in a gorgeous spot, we could see the summit of Bertha. It looked just like pictures I had seen of Mount Everest. After lunch I roped up with Maynard, and while trying to climb a cornice to pose for a picture for Brad, I took another slide.

After climbing for seven hours we were making progress along the main ridge at 8,500 feet. The summit was only about 1,700 vertical feet above us, but we reluctantly decided to turn back at 6:30 p.m. There was no way we could reach the summit before dark and it was no ridge to be fooling around on at night. I was discouraged because I wasn't sure I would have the strength to climb back up on the next clear day.

Turning back was a wise decision, though. Our feet were soaking wet, we were getting colder, and the trip down wasn't going to be easy. Brad tried a shortcut by rappelling straight over a crevasse, but the crevasse was twenty-five feet wide and he didn't like the idea of inexperienced climbers—like me—trying it. Brad suggested I try another spot. I swung on the rope, dangling in midair because I couldn't plant my feet steadily on the side of the icy hill. I was scared to death but was ashamed to admit it. I covered up my fright by laughing almost hysterically. Brad was below watching me and Maynard was above belaying me.

That experience certainly taught me the importance of roping up and gave me confidence in the belaying system. Everyone generally found the incident very amusing. But at dinner, young Lowell Thomas suddenly shouted at Brad, "What were you trying to do to Barbara, kill her?"

CHAPTER 5:
A FIRST ASCENT

FOR THREE DAYS AFTER OUR FIRST attempt at the summit of Mount Bertha, the weather was dreadful. One day it was foggy. The next we had a real northeaster. The tent flapped constantly while pouring rain leaked in on every side. Everything in the tent was wet and we had to huddle together to keep warm. Brad tried to raise our spirits by creating a tiny oven out of a five-gallon fuel can and using it to make toasted cheese on crackers. The air in the tent was so blue with smoke that we were all choking. When we tried to sleep, it was bedlam. Our space was so cramped that every movement was felt along the line. Whenever anyone rolled over, we all rolled over onto the next person, until finally Brad was jammed against the tent wall.

It took until July 30 to get free of the rain and wind and set out for the top of Bertha. We woke at 1:00 a.m. and it didn't look encouraging. We went back to sleep and then examined the weather again at 3:15. It was cloudy, but it looked as if it might clear, so we made breakfast. I was not feeling very chipper, so I was hoping the weather would not improve. But of course it did.

Brad shouted, "Let's go! Everybody up!" We put on our boots, threw

◀ I had reason to smile on July 30, 1940: I was standing on the summit of Alaska's Mount Bertha, with the first climbing party to ever reach the top. *Courtesy of the National Geographic Society*

Courtesy of the National Geographic Society

Here's the successful Mount Bertha summit team. Brad and I are standing behind (from left to right) Maynard Miller, Michl Feuersinger, and Tom Winship.

on our already-packed rucksacks, and hit the trail. I couldn't even swallow any breakfast. I stuffed a few pilot crackers in my pocket, hoping they would sustain me. The climbing conditions were excellent. We walked on frozen snow. At first I was sluggish and was afraid I would be a drag on the group, but I gradually felt better. Sneaking bites of pilot crackers definitely improved my morale.

We reached a food cache at 8:00 a.m. and stopped for a meal. We actually had to descend a short way. Then came an interminable uphill rock scramble. And then it was down into another pass. We were in fog most of the way. But then the fog vanished and we had a magnificent view of nearby Mount Crillon, which Brad had climbed in 1934.

We ascended what seemed an endless ridge to reach Bertha's plateau—an undulating field of fresh powder snow, offering views of Crillon and La Perouse and, in the distance, the top of Mount Fairweather. We had a marvelous look at Bertha's summit, the final cone rising higher as we came nearer. It looked like just a step to the top, even if it was still a fairly long way. Fortunately I was able to walk on a layer of crust, not sinking into the snow very often.

That easy traveling ended, though. The final ascent was difficult and exhausting as Win led for our climbing party, which also included Maynard and Michl. We sank in every other step to our knees. We knew we were on top when there was no more uphill. For the first time, Mount Bertha was climbed, and was I ever relieved to have made it!

We reached the summit at 3:30 in the afternoon and the view from the top was almost beyond description. We looked down on a sea of cumulus clouds, great puffy masses piled up on the distant horizon. Brady Glacier was partly covered with fog, but you could see shadows through it on the snow below. Hugh Miller Inlet was visible through the clouds and its blue water seemed welcoming. We could look across at mighty 15,000-foot Fairweather and down at Johns Hopkins Glacier, dirty with avalanche debris.

Reaching the summit was emotional for all of us. It had been our destination for so long and had seemed so far away. I was so glad I had been able to make it to the top. I certainly wasn't any great athlete or mountaineer, but I had learned on the job We were terribly lucky with the weather. The summit had not even been visible for days, but when we were on top it was warm and windless. We had a group hug, a picture-taking orgy, and displayed the American flag and the National Geographic Society flag.

Just as we were about to leave the summit, Win announced that he had to relieve himself. That gave me courage, so I announced that I had the same need. But we were all very modest and there were no trees to hide behind. Brad responded, "No problem, we have lots of rope." He tied the rope around Win's waist and let him down one steep side of the summit, then tied the rope around my waist and let me down the other side. As I was relieving myself, looking out over such magnificent scenery, I began to laugh uncontrollably. What would my friends at home think of this sight?

As we shouldered our packs and began the descent, I turned around for one last look at the view from the summit because I knew I would never be there again. The trip down was worse than the trip up at times, but also easier in some ways. Our legs were tired and there were uphill areas to traverse, but I was more relaxed and was actually enjoying myself. We got back to the food cache just before dark. From there we used flashlights at times, and coming down a ridge with that as the only light was no fun. There was blue ice beneath the snow.

We reached camp at 12:45 a.m.—on the trail for nineteen hours and forty minutes. I was so fatigued I couldn't eat, and simply drank a cup of lemonade. That was my big celebration.

The next morning we were a sorry sight. We slept very late and were looking forward to a special breakfast of cocoa and sardines, the things we longed for on the climb. Now the cocoa seemed too rich and the sardines went begging. Our appetites had pretty much disappeared. Nothing that we could produce seemed appealing.

At 3:00 p.m., Brad, Michl, and I began our descent to base camp. It was not a pleasant trip. The snow was icy and several of the snow bridges we used on the way up had melted. It took three hours and I felt as if I had reached Nirvana when we stopped. The dogs greeted us with enthusiastic barking, the cook tent was neat as a pin, and Lowell, Alva, and Lee were happy to see us. Best of all, Brad and I now had a tent of our own.

When we awoke the next morning we were in a real rainstorm. It almost made us happy, though, because we needed a chance to rest. It never occurred to us that Win and Maynard, higher up the mountain, would attempt to descend to base camp in such weather, but around noon we heard a loud whistle up on the ridge and there they were, working their way slowly down. The weather was even worse up high, and they didn't want to be there any longer.

The following day, August 1, was the laziest of the trip. It poured rain,

Brad and I showed off the American flag and the flag of the National Geographic Society after succeeding in the first ascent of Mount Bertha. *Photo by Tom Winship*

so I snuggled into my sleeping bag and dozed until 5:00 p.m. We then made plans for our trip across Brady Glacier and down to Reid Inlet. After a good night's sleep, we awoke at 6:00 a.m. to prepare for sledging the dogs a dozen miles across Brady Glacier.

Although the weather was foggy and misty, we decided to press on with the dogs and get them as far as we could. We had some difficulty getting the sled over some big crevasses. At 7:00 p.m., after traveling twelve miles, we found a beautiful campsite at the base of lush, green mountains that reminded me of the highlands of northern Scotland. Fortified by a supper of macaroni and cheese, we walked up onto a rock ridge close to camp. From there we could look down toward Reid Inlet and tidewater. What a wonderful thing to see after being on snow and ice for so long.

We rose at dawn the next day, put on heavy loads, and headed down-glacier. In two hours we were within signaling distance of a mine that was in the area. As we came over the brow of a hill, we saw two men far below us prospecting in the rocks of the glacial moraine. We shot our pistol three times and they came up to meet us. We walked with the two prospectors—Joe Ibach and a Swede named Nels—to their skiff, and inside was a large supply of apples, cookies, and chocolate bars, which they shared with us. Suddenly that lost appetite was regained. I never enjoyed an apple so much in my life.

We spent the next week collecting all of our supplies from abandoned caches and waiting for good weather. Brad needed the weather in order to make a photographic flight on a seaplane that would come from Juneau. On August 12 the weather cleared, the plane arrived, and we had a wonderful flight as Brad took scores of aerial photographs of Mount Bertha, Mount Fairweather, and the nearby glaciers.

We led a busy social life as we waited for Ginky Bayers and his fishing boat *Forester* to take us back to Juneau. We received a surprising visit from a Mr. and Mrs. Stuart, who were cruising Hugh Miller Inlet in their private boat and invited us on a thrilling ride. Their Chris-Craft cruised at thirty-five miles an hour, and it felt like traveling in a Rolls Royce. We

Alva Morrison, right, and Tom Winship were happy to get the coffee I served at Reid Inlet at the conclusion of our Mount Bertha climb.

continued through thick pack ice almost to the end of John Hopkins Inlet. Then we raced up Tarr Inlet to Margery Glacier, with its vertical wall of ice at the snout. Suddenly huge chunks of turquoise-colored ice calved into the water, causing us to back off to a safer viewing spot. When the glacier stopped its spectacular show, we sped back to our camp, freezing all the way.

Muz Ibach, Joe's wife, insisted that Brad and I sleep in her cabin. She said she could sleep on their boat. We accepted her invitation enthusiastically, but the bunk turned out to be too narrow for both of us and I woke up with a backache. At least the cabin was warmer than our tent. We used the stove there to make a cake for miner Tom Smith's birthday, his sixty-fourth.

When Kinky and the *Forester* showed up, we hastily loaded our supplies on board and said our farewells and the *Forester* pulled away from shore under a heaven of brilliant stars and Northern Lights. Muz came with us so that we could let her off at Lemesurier Island, where she and Joe had a beautiful home surrounded by a spectacular garden. I shall never forget the sight of that pretty, petite lady standing on the shore, waving goodbye to us and shouting, "Don't feel sorry for the one who's left behind! I feel sorry for you!" For leaving Alaska, she meant. Alaska had many of these plucky, pioneer ladies who followed their husbands to live in the wilderness.

After this melancholy parting, we all settled down to read the piles of mail Kinky brought for us. But our abiding interest was food—perhaps a delayed reaction to all the calories we burned on the climb. I was ravenous. For breakfast I had three fried eggs, six slices of bacon, four pieces of toast, jam, coffee, and an orange. Brad had the same, only he had five eggs! For supper we happily downed a meal of mashed potatoes, roast beef and gravy, carrots, peas, and lettuce and tomato salad.

We arrived in Juneau early on the morning of August 15 and immediately headed for the Gastineau Hotel. What a luxurious feeling, sleeping on clean, white sheets. The next morning we had breakfast with two Juneau newspapermen who wanted to hear the story of our climb. Then Brad got cornered in a barber shop and was persuaded to agree to giving a lecture to the Chamber of Commerce.

Despite all of these experiences to engage me, I had not been feeling well for days. I thought I probably was just getting the grippe, and it would go away by itself. But an old friend of Brad's, a Dr. Council, practiced in Juneau, and Brad urged me to see him. Dr. Council apparently took care of everyone in Juneau, because there was a long line of patients waiting to see him.

He took me in and looked me over briefly, then opened his door and called out to Brad: "Hell, there's nothing wrong with this girl, she's just pregnant!"

That evening Brad and I had a farewell party with the rest of our group and I told them my news. Tommy Winship took exception to this development. "Barbara!" he exclaimed. "How could you be pregnant? I was sleeping beside you most of the time."

We were up very early on August 16 to give the boys a gala sendoff on the *Princess Charlotte*. Brad and I were leaving later, aboard the *Prince Rupert*, so we made one more photo flight with pilot Alex Holden. We flew across the Fairweather Range and Brad pointed out his route in making the first ascent of Mount Crillon, in 1934. We tried to fly over the summit of Mount Bertha, but the air was too rough.

The *Prince Rupert* was due to depart at 12:40 a.m., but when we were dumped at the dock with all of our baggage, including seven dogs, there was no sign of the boat. Because of fog we didn't depart until 4:30. On the morning of August 19, the boat docked in Prince Rupert, British Columbia, where we caught the train for Montreal. On the last day of the trip home, we found ourselves on a Canadian National train along with many refugees from Europe. Two people from Austria told us about their escape and boat trip to North America. World War II was imminent.

We were met at White River Junction, New Hampshire, by Brad's sister, Mabel Colgate, who arrived driving a station wagon so we could load the dogs. We caused a sensation when we arrived at Rockywold Camp on Squam Lake, where Brad's parents were spending the summer. We tied the dogs to trees in the woods next to the cottage. Many of Brad's friends and relatives had not met me before. "So you're the new bride," they would say. "You don't look like a mountain climber."

I wanted to say something like, "I'm not, but I did get to the top of Mount Bertha—and it was a first ascent." But I didn't say anything. I did not attach a great deal of importance to the achievement at the time, though I eventually came to learn that many mountaineers did. My family was also very proud of me for making it to the top. I didn't talk much about the trip to my friends. To them it would have been as if I had gone to the moon.

CHAPTER Six

SOUL-SEARCHING

By THE TIME I GOT HOME from climbing Mount Bertha, I was three months pregnant. Our daughter Dorothy was born on March 7, 1941.

Brad and I were extremely proud parents, showing off our new daughter to family and friends at every opportunity. The young addition to our family, though, seemed likely to change our lives considerably. We would no longer be so free to travel. At the same time, Brad's job at the museum became more demanding. At one point I hired a helper so I could audit a course in geology at Harvard, but most of my time was spent being a stay-at-home mother, and I thoroughly enjoyed it.

Then one day in April, Brad turned to me with a surprising idea. "Surely we are going to be involved in this war," he said of the conflict in Europe. "This summer may be our last chance to make a trip to Alaska, maybe forever. So we ought to plan an expedition to get more lecture material."

Most of our income came from Brad's articles for *National Geographic* and other publications and from his lectures. The museum job provided less than half our income. I had very mixed emotions when Brad broached the idea. I knew how much he wanted me to share his experiences, but how in the world could I leave our baby?

Trying to decide the right thing to do was very trying for me. I endured a great deal of soul-searching, but finally decided I should attempt to share

Brad's life as much as possible. If I was going to adhere to that philosophy for the lifetime of our marriage, I knew it would mean making some difficult choices along the way. Whether to leave Dotty behind for an Alaska expedition would be the first one.

As part of my deliberations I consulted our pediatrician. But I received no advice in determining how harmful it might be to leave a child so young for an extended period. In those days we heard no talk about the importance of bonding. And if I were to go, who would Dotty stay with?

Screwing up my courage, I turned to my mother. My father had died of a heart attack when Dotty was only two weeks old and I naively thought my mother would be thrilled to take care of my little baby, her first grandchild—that it would keep her from being lonely. I was mistaken. My mother said she had just signed up for a course in choral conducting at Tanglewood in western Massachusetts. In retrospect I wonder how I could have thought that baby-sitting for me would have been the right thing for her at that time in her life. My mother was not yet sixty and was full of pep, with many interests and talents. Even though she couldn't volunteer as a baby-sitter, my mother never said a word in criticism about me leaving Dotty behind.

I had to work up my courage again and try elsewhere. I turned to Brad's parents, who were a great deal older than my mother. They were going to spend the summer at Rockywold Camp on Squam Lake, where all household chores were taken care of, so I felt that Dotty would not be too much for them. We could hire a nurse to help out. They seemed happy to take on the responsibility. Part of it, I'm sure, is that they knew their son well enough to understand that if he could not get away to do his thing and be able to earn that critically needed income from lecturing, he would be unhappy. I got the impression, too, that they were glad Brad had a wife who was willing to share his adventures. They didn't express it quite that way, but they were always paying me compliments about how I helped in his life.

We found a capable young woman to help out with Dotty, and on June 24, 1941, they all set out by car for Squam Lake. I felt that under the care of the grandparents, and with the help of the nurse, Dotty would do fine. Seeing Dotty leave was a terrible wrench for me, but once I made the decision to travel with Brad, I knew I had to concentrate on being a good companion. We had been working so hard on preparations for the trip that it was almost a relief to know Dotty was in good hands so we could attend to last-minute details.

This expedition would take us to Mount Hayes, a 13,740-foot mountain in the Alaska Range, about ninety miles from Fairbanks. Like Mount Bertha, Mount Hayes had never been climbed. Our itinerary called for us to travel by train across the United States to Seattle, then by boat to Valdez, Alaska. From there we were to travel by truck to Fairbanks, where we would meet the other members of our expedition.

On June 25 we bid farewell to my mother and to Brad's sister and jumped onto the train, praying the porter would make up our berth quickly. We were exhausted. We had an intermission in Minneapolis, staying for two days with relatives of Brad's, who offered rest and recreation. We needed that, but we did miss Dotty so much.

After two pleasant days of swimming and tennis, we boarded a train again. On this part of the trip I noted in my journal how much greener the prairies were and how black and rich the soil looked compared with the land of Western Canada, which we crossed the previous summer as we traveled back and forth to Mount Bertha. I also noted that we had a delicious roast beef dinner for seventy-five cents.

We arrived in Seattle on the morning of June 30 and were met by Ome Daiber, a climbing friend. Ome was the inventor of Sno-Seal, a waterproofing product for leather boots that is still in use today. With his help we bought supplies, then socialized with other friends. We woke at 6:00 a.m. to catch the boat bound for Valdez. Brad had a wretched cold, so he immediately snuggled into a lower berth. I enjoyed the magnificent scenery as we sailed past Vancouver and headed up Georgia Strait.

I was going north to Alaska again.

The next morning was beautiful and clear. We were in open ocean and the boat had a real roll for several hours, but we managed not to get seasick.

After a brief stop in Ketchikan, Alaska, we sailed through the Wrangell Narrows and enjoyed a superb sunset. The look of the tiny town of Petersburg, nestled below snowcapped peaks, reminded me of the story of the Swiss girl Heidi that I read as a child. We were met in Juneau by friends of Brad, who drove us out of town to see the Mendenhall Glacier—even then a popular destination for visitors. The Fourth of July arrived, but it was no fun for me as I fought a cold while everyone else was noisily celebrating the nation's birthday.

After leaving Juneau, we hoped to catch a glimpse of the Fairweather Range, where Brad had done so much climbing and exploring in the early 1930s. Unfortunately, Mount Fairweather and Mount Crillon looked more like clouds than mountains. In Cordova, Brad brought me to see a friend of his, Smitty, a bush pilot he had flown with in years past. It was very early in the morning, but we walked to Smitty's house and surprised him still in bed. After bear hugs and shouts of joy, Brad and Smitty reminisced about their flights together. It was fascinating to listen to them because I didn't know a lot about Brad's earlier adventures in Alaska.

Sailing again in the afternoon, we passed the Columbia Glacier, one of the most impressive in Alaska. It was fun to see the expressions of awe on the faces of passengers who were seeing their first glacier. They asked Brad so many questions about glaciers that he finally agreed to give a lecture on the subject that evening. I found that I, as well as the tourists, learned a great deal more about glaciers from his talk than I knew before.

Late on the afternoon of July 6, our boat arrived in Valdez, then a very small, rundown town. Our truck driver, Paul Chamberlain, found us and said we would be leaving at midnight. We were sleepy, but the excitement of adventure kept us going. We loaded eight tons of freight on the truck, which was also transporting 9,600 bottles of beer.

We climbed into the front seat beside Paul, and with a full moon shining on the snow-covered hills, headed up the Richardson Highway to Fairbanks. I was terribly excited. This was a completely new part of Alaska for me. The midnight sun shone through most of the night. My body kept wanting to doze, but my mind kept urging me to stay awake so I wouldn't miss anything. We passed ski slopes and tremendous waterfalls.

We stopped for breakfast at Gulkana, at a typical log-cabin Alaska road-house, where we ate family-style with other truckers. The roadhouses in this part of Alaska were constructed around the turn of the twentieth century and spaced just far enough apart for a dog driver to mush his team for a day's worth of travel, then spend a sheltered night.

Next stop, Delta, where we crossed the Tanana River on a ferry. The final part of the journey was over roadway that was bumpy, torn up, and muddy. We pulled into Fairbanks at 10:00 p.m., twenty-two hours after leaving Valdez, still in broad daylight. We gave ourselves an ice cream as a reward, then collapsed into bed in the Pioneer Hotel and slept for twelve hours.

The next day our bush pilot, Johnny Lynn, suggested flying to Mount Hayes to scout out a safe landing spot for the expedition. Good idea, but unsuc-cessful. We ran into a rain squall about twenty minutes out and had to turn back. I spent the afternoon packing cereal into food bags for the climb while Brad worked on an article for the Royal Geographical Society of London.

The following morning we flew out of Fairbanks with Johnny for the one-hour flight to Mount Hayes. It was cloudy over the mountain, but we eventually glimpsed a small gravel landing strip on Delta Creek that had been built by gold prospectors. The field was short, and it made for a scary landing. We climbed out of the plane and found a place for base camp beside a clear stream, surrounded by a beautiful forest. Our enthusiasm dampened as soon as the mosquitoes began to bite. Alaska has a fearsome reputation for voracious bugs and these mosquitoes lived up to it.

Taking off again, we circled in close to the base of Mount Hayes to find the best place for airdropping supplies. We needed good landing spots for the parachutes that would be used to cushion the free-fall of our supplies being thrown out from above.

We also examined the best way to climb onto the summit ridge. We flew up through cotton-like, puffy clouds, and suddenly the white summit of Hayes loomed up, all clear against an azure sky. The mountain was breath-taking in appearance, and the narrow, steep, corniced ridge leading to the top was truly intimidating. I couldn't imagine myself on that ridge. We studied the mountain from all sides, and Brad meticulously observed the route he had chosen based on the aerial photos he had taken in 1936.

We spent the next few days in Fairbanks. The town offered plenty of local color. I had never heard such a racket as that coming from down in the bar, with its crowd of drunks. We packed more food and supplies, searched for parachutes, and argued about what kind of plane was most appropriate to use for our airdrops. Eventually we used both a Cessna and an Army plane. The Army's agreement to drop stuff to us from a bomber was welcome. The Army also sent Captain Robin Montgomery with us to learn about parachute dropping of equipment in the wilderness and about the cold-weather clothing and gear being used in Alaskan mountaineering.

At our base camp, I and the other climbers prepared for our 1941 ascent of Mount Hayes, a peak in the Alaska Range that had yet to be climbed.

Chapter Seven

THE MARCH UP MOUNT HAYES

ROBIN, BRAD, AND I FLEW OFF for our Mount Hayes base camp on the morning of July 15. Upon landing, the first thing we did was set up the radio. Then we unpacked the tents and did our best to organize a camp for comfortable living.

The mosquitoes were so aggressive the next morning that we tried to escape by taking a dip in the nearby stream. The icy water quickly drove us back into the tent to warm up. That evening while we were cooking supper, we heard the roar of a plane. We rushed out to watch Johnny land and drop off Ben Ferris and Bill Shand, two members of our expedition who had been working in Fairbanks to organize the supply drop. Like all members of our party, they were experienced climbers. They had the supplies packed in layers of protection: Goods were inside bags, which were packed inside boxes, which were packed inside sturdier containers.

Anxious to establish a second camp as soon as possible, we set out on a trek to higher elevation at 10:00 p.m. All that I could manage at that time was thirty pounds, but the others carried sixty-pound loads. The first half hour of walking through timber was easy, but when we struck a swamp of nothing but tussocks, we all slowed down. The northern sky of summer granted us views of both sunset and sunrise. It was after midnight when we set up our tent beside Caribou Creek. Robin insisted on sleeping on the

ground outside the tent, but later he came crawling inside to seek refuge from the mosquitoes.

It was warm, and we rose at 8:00 a.m. after a fairly sleepless night of scratching and sweating. Brad and I shared one sleeping bag because that was all we could carry on the first relay. By late morning we were on our way again, and the walking became easier when we got to the crest of a ridge. We stopped for lunch at a spot overlooking a picturesque lake, where our rest was interrupted by a downpour and wind squall. Moving on in spite of high wind, we soon found a comfortable spot to spend the night. A young caribou walked by as we were setting up the tent and gave us a thorough going-over before leaping away.

We pushed on the next morning to the green patch of ground that we had selected as the site for our first airdrop. We scarcely had time to lay out a signal panel when we heard the hum of a Douglas bomber in the distance. Just as the plane approached our target, a terrific wind came up and it began to hail. In spite of the very low ceiling, the crew threw out one parachute with four gas cans tied together. The plane flew so low that the chute barely had time to open. On the second pass, the box that was dropped burst on impact and cans of jam scattered everywhere. The airplane crew dropped a note saying they would return later—but before leaving, they dropped one more load. Everything landed a long way off the target.

When the plane returned later, the crew did a better job of hitting the target, and the parachutes landed perfectly. The crew dropped another note, this one with some bad news about a beer keg. We had filled two kegs with gasoline for the expedition. One of the kegs, the note said, had accidentally fallen out the door of the plane. The crew enclosed a map showing where the accident occurred. Since the spot was five miles away, we gave up any thought of retrieving that keg. The second keg of gasoline landed perfectly, right near our tent.

Later in the afternoon, Ben and Bill headed back down the route to retrieve supplies to be dropped from the Cessna. While Brad and I cooked supper, we heard the motor of the plane and I laughed at a mental image of Ben and Bill scurrying around to gather up the stuff being dropped. An icy wind was roaring outside the tent, but the summit of Mount Hayes was clear and bathed in sun.

Just a day later it was already time for Robin to leave the expedition. He had to hike all the way back to our landing field with a huge load of parachutes, which were only borrowed from the Army and had to be returned. "I think I'm cheating a packhorse out of a job," he said as he left. We roared with laughter because he looked ridiculous covered with parachutes, the load so awkward he could hardly stand up. We would miss his wonderful sense of humor.

Bill, Ben, Brad, and I started out across the glacier, and I found the walking very rough because the surface was covered with so many loose rocks. But I kept my misery to myself and we arrived at our destination in plenty of time to receive Johnny's prearranged airdrop of sixteen bundles of supplies. Two of the boxes smashed to bits when they hit the ground. Our breakfast biscuits were pulverized. Prunes scattered in every direction.

That night I had a heavenly sleep. At long last my own sleeping bag had caught up with me, carried on someone's back on our last relay. Then I had a wonderful day by myself as Brad, Ben, and Bill walked back to our previous camp to fetch more supplies. I was supposed to supervise another plane bombardment, but Johnny's Cessna never showed up.

I took Ben's binoculars, and for amusement I walked up the rock slope behind camp and spotted Brad and the others starting their return hike. Back in our tent, tidying up, I lifted the tent flap to see if the boys were near, but instead I saw three snow-white Dall sheep staring at me. They were a beautiful sight silhouetted against the blue sky. As soon as I reached for a camera, they darted away in the fog. I walked over on the knoll and watched four of them eating. It's rare to see these sheep up close like that. More often they are far away, appearing as nothing more than dots on the hillsides.

Brad and his companions reappeared, accompanied by the last two members of our party to be flown in: Henry Hall, of Cambridge, an officer of the American Alpine Club who was about sixty years old, and climber Sterling Hendricks. Ben had a broad smile on his face as he handed me a bird he had bagged—a ptarmigan, a kind of grouse found in northern regions. I plucked it and Ben cleaned it and then made ptarmigan stew for himself for supper—though the small bird provided barely enough food to whet his appetite. While enjoying supper with the two newest members of our group, we listened for the sound of Johnny's plane. This was the first really clear evening we had had for a long time, so we thought he might show up for the next airdrop. But no plane.

The next morning we headed out on a day trek and were some distance from camp when we heard the distant hum of an airplane. We realized, to our dismay, that Johnny was dumping our stuff from his plane with no one in camp to direct the drop. But when we returned to camp, we discovered that all the bundles had landed safely. We were fortunate. Now, able to relax, we spent the afternoon reading and puttering around.

After supper we walked up to a spot where Oscar Houston, who tried to climb Mount Hayes in 1937, had left a cache. We found the cache in an advanced state of deterioration, but in the midst of the pile we discovered the packboard of Oscar's son, Charlie. It was the same packboard Charlie had used on Brad's Mount Crillon expedition in 1933, and Brad got a huge kick out of finding this relic of a previous adventure.

Our next goal was to establish our first advanced camp, at 8,500 feet. We climbed a long gully with horribly loose rocks until we reached snow. It took us about four hours to reach the site of the advanced camp, and I was the first to get there—surprised by my own stamina. But it was disconcerting to see the steepness of the ridge we were going to have to climb to reach the summit. It held lots of loose powder snow.

The descent from the new campsite was a cinch for everyone but me and Henry. The others glissaded all the way down the gully, in a fast and controlled slide to the bottom. But Henry and I didn't know how to glissade. We had to move much more slowly and carefully as we walked downward, and my crampons kept filling with snow. "My hand is still shaking from descending the long slope behind camp," I wrote in my diary. "My feet and legs are aching, and I'm very relieved to be back in camp."

We ended the evening with a spirited argument over whether there was value in training mountain troops for the Army.

After two days of sitting in camp because of windy weather, we made another trip to our 8,500-foot advanced camp. I felt miserable all the way up the rocky part of the slope, carrying my thirty-pound pack—and I felt even worse when we hit the snow. At the same time, the boys were carrying ninety-pound packs. I thought it was silly to pretend we were enjoying ourselves doing this backbreaking work.

As a distraction from my discomfort, I went through mental exercises, planning make-believe dinner parties. I worked out the menus and decided which interesting people would come and who would sit next to whom. Being very practical, I did not imagine inviting famous people, just professors we knew back home in Massachusetts. All this planning was a marvelous diversion. That evening as I cooked supper on the Primus stove, falling snow made a pleasing sound on the roof of our cozy tent. In spite of my distress when I was enduring the climb, I realized the companionship and the adventure were indeed worth the struggle.

We spent the next two days trying to relay supplies to a higher cache at about 9,000 feet. Snow and fog impeded progress, although one superb clear-off gave us a spectacular view of the alabaster-like ridge leading to the summit. Hastily we grabbed our packs to take advantage of this interlude of clear weather and reached the next campsite in only two hours. Except for two icy pitches, the going was fairly easy.

Our window of clear weather evaporated swiftly. The next day we were hit by fresh snowstorms. Brad, Sterling, and Henry ignored the worsening weather and left in the fog to carry loads upward. The other climbers

The route from our final camp took us up over the north shoulder of Mount Hayes, then along the narrow, corniced ridge leading toward the summit.

relayed supplies to 8,500 from the camp below. When they all returned later in the day, the snow began falling faster and heavier. It seemed like a good idea to snuggle into our sleeping bags and catch up on needed rest.

It was still snowing the next morning and the temperature inside the tent was only 22 degrees. We needed to keep supplies moving up, so we headed off anyway. It took us three and a half hours of wading knee-deep in powder snow to reach the upper cache, using three fixed ropes to help us over one steep, icy spot. Occasionally we had to kick entirely new steps because of the fresh snow. With that snow still steadily falling, we couldn't see a thing all the way.

The next day was gorgeous. I guess it was a reward for having the patience to trudge through the deep snow. It was 11:00 a.m. when we broke camp and started up the ridge, aiming for a campsite at 9,000 feet. We moved very slowly. The views were more impressive than anything from Mount Bertha the year before because of the sharpness of the ridge and the precipitous peaks close around us. It was also lovely to be able to look out at green valleys instead of simply facing white mountains as far as the eye could see. During the previous few days it had snowed almost as far down as the landing field, so huge white patches of white decorated the greensward.

We reached the campsite at 5:00 p.m. and drank in the view for a long time. The temperature was 18 degrees and falling rapidly. There was no wind, however, so it didn't feel any colder than it had lower on the mountain. We watched a spectacular sunset over a thick sea of clouds, then saw a new moon appear over Mount McKinley, many miles to the west. How could I possibly imagine that in six years I would be standing on that very summit?

Courtesy of the National Geographic Society

The final section of the route up Mount Hayes traveled the precipitous ridge from the mountain's north shoulder (at far right) to the steep summit snowfields.

Courtesy of the National Geographic Society

The ascent of Mount Hayes turned out to be more challenging than the climb of Mount Bertha the year before. Here I'm at the 9,000-foot elevation on Hayes.

CHAPTER 8 *Eight*
JOY AT THE SUMMIT

OUR NEXT OBJECTIVE WAS THE SUMMIT. We were at our high camp and there was only one stop left—the 13,740-foot top of Mount Hayes.

On July 29, Brad crawled out of the tent at 6:00 a.m. to observe the weather. It was a fairly good day, but he didn't think it would stay clear for long, so he tried to persuade us to be patient and wait for a better day. But the gang was raring to go. Since Henry was the oldest, Brad let him decide whether we should make a dash for the summit. Henry thought it over, then said, "Let's go!"

The weather wasn't bad at all when we left camp at 8:30 a.m. or as we climbed. But after endless wallowing in deep powder snow, with Brad, Bill, and Sterling taking turns leading, we finally got up to 12,800 feet and had a caucus. Henry, on the rope with me and Brad, complained that we were going too fast. Brad said we would have to move even faster or turn back because of an approaching storm. Henry said he couldn't go any faster, so Sterling took him on his rope. We decided to keep going, with a sharp eye on the weather.

I was really frightened by the idea of a storm blowing in and forcing us to make a dash to camp for safety. However, I also felt that the summit looked closer than it ever might again. After making a little more progress, we had another discussion, and we all agreed we should turn back. The clouds were piling up rapidly. It was a bitter disappointment to give up when the summit seemed so near.

We retreated to camp. Eating supper lifted our gloomy moods. When the snow began falling, we realized we had made the right decision and were happy to be in our cozy tents.

The following day we faced snow squalls and gale winds. It was 22 degrees, but felt colder. Henry and Ben dug a cave. I sewed Henry's pants and read. We did have a gorgeous sunset.

The weather still wasn't good enough to make the climb the next day. Some of us relaxed, but Brad put a fixed rope on the steep pitch above camp in preparation for our blitz of the mountain. Even though the summit was clear for a short time, we were smart enough to not try climbing in the howling wind. We played cards all evening and went to bed with one eye on the weather.

Brad woke at 3:00 a.m. and peeked out to check the weather. He nearly had his head torn off by a gale and its blasting snow. He checked again at 4:00, but it was still not good. He tried again at 5:00 and the weather looked more promising. So he got us all organized, except for Henry, who didn't feel he could go—it just wasn't his day. So the other five of us departed at 6:30. It was now August 1.

The steps previously chopped and the fixed rope on the steep section above camp helped tremendously, so we climbed much faster than on the first attempt. We took a short snack break before tackling some sharp pinnacles with precarious cornices just above where we lunched on the last try. The sun appeared periodically, and the summit was visible as we came out above a sea of heavy clouds.

The ridge between the 12,000-foot shoulder and the summit of Hayes is spectacular—extremely narrow and exposed. The difficult ridge required all of our attention. As we approached a cornice I was told, "All right, Barbara, you go first because you're light."

They put me first on the rope to test the cornices along the ridge, figuring that if I fell because the overhanging snow of the cornice collapsed, they could hold me easily on the rope with their strength and weight. I tried to appear calm and confident, but I was really trembling with fear as I climbed ahead. This was much more of a climbing challenge than I had faced the previous year on Mount Bertha. But I did not slip and none of the cornices gave way, and everyone followed safely behind me. Above this thrilling part of the climb, the last thousand feet of the ascent was simply a long, exhausting trudge.

We stepped onto the summit of Mount Hayes at 1:45 in the afternoon. The fellows pulled rolls of colored paper and confetti out of their pockets and waved them around in a frenzy of joy. It was like being at a wedding reception. It was 11 degrees and there was an icy wind, but I was dressed for it. I was wearing a boy's parka that I had bought back home, with some bunny fur that I had sewed onto the edge. I also wore long winter underwear, wool pants, and two wool shirts. In the boy's parka, I looked ten years old.

There is a certain pride in making a first ascent, especially when others had tried before you and not succeeded. This mountain was climbed again years later, but everyone on that expedition expressed great respect for what we had done with our old-fashioned equipment in 1941.

We remained on the summit for almost an hour, taking pictures frantically. Before the weather closed in, we had beautiful views of the Cathedral Mountains, the Susitna Glacier, and the south shoulder of our mountain. We left the summit just in time, because clouds rolled in and we descended the sharp pinnacles of the ridge in dense fog.

We arrived back in camp tired but happy after twelve long hours of climbing. The entry in my diary for August 1 reads: "Our goal has been achieved. Mount Hayes has been climbed for the first time!"

The next morning, after a long bull session, we decided that Henry, Brad, and I would walk back down to the landing field while the other three fellows established a cache of stuff near the bottom of Kimrea, a 12,000-foot mountain just east of Hayes. Their plan was to climb Kimrea, then meet us at the landing field with the rest of our gear before we returned to Fairbanks.

Our trio left at 4:30 in the afternoon and hiked for five hours. We had to deal with bad slush and ice part of the way, and I had difficulty keeping my crampons on. The worst part was descending the shale slope above our old base camp with forty-two pounds on my back. Crossing the glacier was easy, but we ran into fog just after we hit the greensward, and the tussocks underfoot were troublesome. Brad and I favored stopping there but Henry, with a lighter load, kept floating along. It took harsh words from us to persuade him we needed a break.

The fog blocked our view, but with the help of a map we figured we were about halfway to the landing field. I was so tired and disgusted from slipping on rocks and sliding off tussocks that I couldn't have gone much farther. In twenty minutes we had set up a comfortable campsite and began drying out our pants and socks.

The fog lifted the following morning and we completed the trek back to the landing field. We put up the tent and had a huge lunch of Army C-rations— hash and vegetable stew. Brad set up the radio, and to our amazement reached Fairbanks immediately. The contact was too good to be true. But the reception faded quickly, so we had to guess that Johnny would fly in to pick us up the next afternoon. We felt lucky we were able to get through at all.

By the time the scheduled pickup was due, the weather had turned bad, so we huddled in the tent and settled down for a snooze. The radio was no help, so we couldn't find out if Johnny was coming for us. No sooner had we closed our eyes than we heard the sound of the plane and rushed out to greet it. Within half an hour we had dismantled the tent, clambered aboard the plane, and were on our way to Fairbanks.

One of the joys of returning from an expedition is sleeping between clean sheets. Another is to go to a hairdresser and get fixed up—then you feel completely renewed. In Fairbanks we also visited friends, went to the movies, and treated ourselves to a chocolate sundae. We received a wire of congratulations from Brad's father and one from the National Geographic Society. We had a little celebration in our room with some friends and a bottle of sherry.

We now had a completely different kind of base camp and we used our free time to take photo flights over the Alaska Range. On one four-hour flight over the entire area, I wrote, "Superb view of Mount McKinley the whole way. It is a gigantic mass of mountain, even from 150 miles away." I did not think about the possibility of climbing it at that time. Then came a happy reunion as Bill, Ben, and Sterling rejoined us after their successful climb of Kimrea.

There was no such thing as scheduled flights to the East Coast. Our trip home to Boston involved a lot of hopping around. We flew out of Fairbanks on August 18 for Whitehorse, Yukon. From Whitehorse we flew to Fort St. John, British Columbia. Then it was Grande Prairie, Alberta, and on to Edmonton, Alberta. As I was walking through a revolving door of our hotel lobby in Edmonton, I ran into Lauritz Melchior, the opera star we had lunch with in Juneau a year before. He was once again on a hunting trip, and here we were once again on a mountaineering expedition.

A pilot friend of ours was ferrying an empty plane to Winnipeg for radio repair and invited us to fly with him instead of taking the train. As we flew toward Winnipeg, the co-pilot asked us if we would like a Coke. Hot and thirsty, we were happy to take him up on the offer. But when the soft drinks didn't arrive, we wondered why the delay. All of a sudden the plane descended and landed at a small airport in Saskatoon. The co-pilot jumped out, walked over to a Coke machine, deposited some coins, and climbed back into the plane with two bottles of Coke for us. Now, that's service.

We flew out of Winnipeg on another flight the next day, changed planes in Fargo, North Dakota, stopped over in Minneapolis, and eventually got back to Boston on August 23.

What a joy it was to hold Dotty in my arms again! She was now five months old—and didn't look as if she had missed us at all. I soon settled down to the routine of motherhood, but with much apprehension about the impending war. We had a fascinating experience on Mount Hayes, but I was very relieved to be home safe and sound. There was going to be a lot to worry about in the coming years.

World War II determined our daily existence for quite some time. Alaska seemed very distant.

CHAPTER *Nine*

WARTIME SEPARATION

THE BOMBING OF PEARL HARBOR on December 7, 1941, changed our lives for the next four years. Brad was assigned to Washington, D.C., to the office of the Quartermaster General. Along with Ad Carter and Bob Bates, two of his friends from the climbing world, Brad was brought in as an expert on cold-weather clothing and survival.

Their first task was to meet with other cold-weather experts who were designing equipment for the Army. I saw Brad off on a train to Washington one day, and he pretty much disappeared from my life for the next three and a half years. I was pregnant with Teddy, so I was relieved Brad was going to Washington and not the battlefield. Little Dotty and I moved to my mother's house, leaving our small apartment behind.

Brad was given a short leave to come home for the birth, but Ted was stubborn and arrived three weeks late. Brad had to return before the birth. Ted was born on September 25, 1942, and weighed over nine pounds. In those days you were given pain medicine that made you lose control of your behavior, and this was a delivery I didn't forget in a hurry. The doctor told me he was shocked to hear such foul language coming from such a refined little lady. I explained to him later that I had been taught the language so I could drive a dog team effectively in Alaska!

While I was in the hospital, I learned of a small house available for rent and was soon strong enough to move into it with the two children. The rent was seventy-five dollars a month and I could just afford it on Brad's Army stipend. I brought Teddy to Washington so Brad could meet his son. We had only one night together, and baby Ted howled most of that time. I had been looking forward to a visit of several days, but the next morning Brad received orders to leave for some secret destination. Disappointed, I returned to Boston, picked up Dotty from Brad's parents, and settled into the new house for the duration. During those difficult years, the grandparents helped enormously, giving me breaks I needed from child rearing.

I tried to join Brad whenever I could, but he usually didn't stay put long. Much of the time I didn't even know where he was. In the spring of 1944, he was transferred to Wright Field in Ohio on a mission for the chief of the Air Force. Since it appeared he would stay there for a while, I moved to Dayton with the children.

We spent a very hot summer in a tiny rented house, but it was wonderful being a family of four, together for the first time. We had some adventures during this period that were far different from our adventures in Alaska. One time we tried to grow tomatoes. Neither one of us had any gardening experience, but we confidently put in the plants and watered them faithfully. Eventually small tomatoes appeared, but they were covered with black spots—dry rot. The tomatoes were totally inedible.

And then I lost Teddy one night. He had a lot of his father's curiosity and he loved to explore the neighborhood. We had no fence around the house, so I usually tied a clothesline around his waist to help keep him close by and safe while I tried to get my housework done. On this particular night, just as dark was approaching, Brad and I went out to the sandbox to get the children ready for bed. To our horror, Teddy was nowhere to be found, and Dotty had no idea where he was. We began to search the neighborhood, Brad in one direction and I in the other, shouting "Teddy!" at the top of our lungs.

We began to panic. Should we call the police? Just as Brad was about to

place the emergency call, I checked in the backyard of a nearby house—
and there was Teddy, sitting peacefully in the neighbors' sandbox, building
beautiful castles. He showed no interest in seeing me. I had to laugh in spite
of my concern. He was a sight. His diaper was down around his ankles, his
face was covered with sand, and he was having an exciting time. He had
untied the clothesline to seek adventure.

In September 1944, Brad was about to be on the move again, on secret
orders, so I picked up the children and returned to Cambridge. I had a baby-
sitter one afternoon a week and used the time to help answer the phone at
a social agency. A group of women formed what we called The Cat Club,
and once a month we met in someone's house after putting our babies to
bed and poured our lonely hearts out to each other. One member of the
group had become pregnant by mistake when her husband was home on a
brief leave. She asked us whether she should write to tell him he was to
be a father for the fourth time. We all agreed he might be so shocked by the
news that it would affect his war work. So the fellow had quite a surprise
when he returned home after the war: He was now the father of four girls.

Brad was home on a short leave in August 1945 when the atomic bomb
was dropped on Japan. We were sitting on a beach on Cape Cod when we
heard the news. I asked, "What in the world is an atom bomb?" To give you
an idea how secretive this horrific military weapon was, Brad said he didn't
have the faintest idea. The Army soon ordered Brad to another unknown
destination, which I learned later was Attu in the Aleutian Islands of Alaska.
He was scheduled to fly from there to Okinawa when the crew chief of the
plane announced that the war was over.

With very little notice, Brad appeared on my doorstep one day in
September 1945. His military service was over. The children didn't really
know their father. They were shy around him at first, but once the ice was
broken they wouldn't let him out of their sight.

One of Brad's Army assignments during World War II was to test cold-
weather gear on Mount McKinley. During the summer of 1942 he took part
in a climb to the summit—only the third ascent in the mountain's history.

The next two years were interesting and happy ones. Brad planned the future of Boston's Museum of Science and I got involved in community affairs, such as the Girl Scouts and the PTA. Betsy was born on June 21, 1946, so I now had three small children to care for, and I often helped Brad with activities at the museum.

One evening, just before Christmas 1946, Brad opened the front door as he usually did each evening around six and yelled "Pennies!" This was a signal for the two older children to make a dash to collect the pennies in Brad's change pocket. When he walked into the kitchen, I noticed an odd expression on his face.

"I had the most extraordinary phone call today," he said. It was from Paul Hollister of RKO Radio Pictures, inviting me to lunch with him at the Ritz. I accepted."

"You can't imagine what he wanted me to do," Brad said. "He asked me to lead an expedition to climb Mount Everest in order to make a short movie that would stimulate interest in mountain climbing in the United States."

RKO was going to make a movie out of James Ramsey Ullman's novel about climbing, *The White Tower*, but the studio was worried the American public wasn't interested in mountaineering. RKO believed an Everest climb and a film about it would excite public attention. Mount Everest, on the border of Nepal and Tibet, had not yet been climbed. Brad said he would love to attempt Mount Everest—but he had to explain that both Nepal and Tibet were closed to westerners.

Instead, Brad proposed to lead a mountaineering expedition to Mount McKinley that could be filmed. It would also give Brad the opportunity he had been seeking to start to make a map of McKinley. Hollister agreed and said RKO would contribute $25,000. That doesn't sound like a great deal of money today, but in those days it would ensure that Brad could invite high-caliber climbers on the trip.

Initially my heart sank at this news because I knew it meant Brad would surely disappear from our lives again, just as the children were getting to know him after his absence during World War II. Then, very quickly, it became apparent that Brad wanted me to be part of the expedition.

The thought of climbing Mount McKinley did not appeal to me. At 20,320 feet, it was a much higher mountain than either Mount Bertha or Mount Hayes, and much colder. Brad had already told me many times after his Army expedition of 1942 just how cold a place Mount McKinley is. My thinking was, "That's beyond me." But Brad knew I could do it. He kept assuring me I could do it.

Then there was the problem of leaving the children. I was not keen on that—and even less so now that we had three young ones. We consulted a pediatrician, who told us he wouldn't expect the kids to be harmed by having their parents go away long enough for the expedition.

Then the movie company got into the act. When they found out I had already done some climbing in Alaska, they said it would make a better movie if a woman was in it. RKO offered to pay for a nurse to live at our house and take care of the children. They put a tremendous amount of pressure on me. After much soul-searching I gave in.

We hired Miss Streeter, a reliable nurse I had known for years. She agreed to move into our house, which would permit the children to stay in their own home, near their school and friends. Both sets of grandparents lived nearby and would make the necessary decisions in case one of the children got sick with something like tonsillitis or another childhood disease. I also asked our children's teachers and the parents of their friends to keep an extra eye on them.

I didn't talk much with anybody outside the immediate family about the fact I was going to Alaska to climb Mount McKinley. It just didn't come up most of the time. One day a woman phoned to ask if I was going to attend the next meeting of the Cambridge Smith College Club. I replied, "No, I'm going to Alaska to climb Mount McKinley." The woman simply said, "Oh," and hung up. Maybe she didn't believe me.

Nobody actually said to me, "How could you go off and leave three children?" But it was a question I had to ask myself. It was very hard for me to leave them. By the time we took off in late March 1947, Dotty was six years old, Teddy was four, and Betsy was nine months.

While we were deep into planning the expedition, I broke out in a rash on my arms and chest. At first I thought I was allergic to wool—which would have been a big problem on McKinley, where it would be impossible to keep warm without wearing wool. But I did not show a response to any of the allergy tests the doctor gave me.

We concluded I was breaking out because of stress and worry about leaving the children. Eventually I was able to feel at peace with my decision. I had decided to go to Mount McKinley with Brad, and I could not torture myself any longer. And whatever the cause of the rash, it soon disappeared.

March 23, 1947, was a happy day with the children. We all had Sunday lunch with Brad's parents, as we usually did. I wrote in my diary:

Gave the children supper and tucked them into bed as if tomorrow would be just another day. It was very difficult for me, knowing that I wouldn't see them for some time. This is probably the most difficult decision I will ever have to make, but Brad seems to want so much to have me share his experiences, I feel I must. I believe I am leaving the children in good hands, and it is a great relief to know there are grandparents nearby.

The view of Mount McKinley's northeast side looks right up the route we took to the top in 1947. The main summit at 20,320 feet is the broad, snowy peak to the left.

CHAPTER Ten
THE CHALLENGE OF MCKINLEY

THAT VERY EVENING WE FLEW to New York. We were met by an RKO limousine, which deposited us at the Commodore Hotel, and in the morning we had breakfast with the president of RKO, Seymour Bergson. At the airport we met Bill Deeke and George Wellsted, the two photographers who would be making the movie of our McKinley climb for RKO. As we boarded the plane, we were surrounded by a horde of newsmen and photographers. We were exhausted, but since we were being sponsored by RKO, we had to put up with the publicity.

We spent the next day in Minneapolis, meeting with more reporters and photographers who wanted to know how we would get stories out to the papers during the expedition. I don't recall much being made of the fact there was a woman on the expedition. I don't think the woman business ever really came up—probably because they didn't believe I'd make it to the summit. In Minneapolis we also met another member of our McKinley party, Hugo Victoreen of Chicago, who would be conducting cosmic ray studies for the Office of Naval Research.

We were scheduled to take off for Anchorage at 1:15 a.m. We were so fatigued that we decided to take sleeping pills to ensure some rest on the flight. I had never taken a sleeping pill and was apprehensive about how my body would react to it. By the time the plane took off at 2:30, I was a zombie. And I did get a few hours of totally restful sleep.

Our plane set down in Edmonton, Alberta, to change pilots and gas up. Then we flew north over Canada into Southeast Alaska. The weather was clear, so Brad had the thrill of seeing his old friends Mount Lucania and Mount Sanford. He had been in the first-ascent party on 17,150-foot Mount Lucania in 1937 and on the first ascent of 16,200-foot Mount Sanford in 1938.

We landed in Anchorage on March 27 and met up with Shorty Lange, Jim Gale, and Bill Hackett, three more members of the expedition. At eighteen, Shorty was the youngest in our group, but he had been recommended to us as a good climber and backpacker. Jim Gale, who was thirty-eight, was "Top Sergeant" with the 10th Air Force's Emergency Rescue Squadron in Alaska and made some daring rescues during the war. Bill Hackett, who was in his early twenties, was a lieutenant in the Army who dreamed of climbing McKinley and who had the courage to write and beg us to take him along when he heard about the expedition. His letter was so persuasive that Brad and I agreed he deserved a chance to prove himself—which he did.

George Browne was also part of the crew. Brownie, in his early twenties, was the son of Belmore Browne, an artist and an old friend of Brad's who made a mark climbing on Mount McKinley in the early part of the twentieth century. On a 1912 expedition, Belmore Browne and Herschel Parker nearly became the first men ever to climb McKinley. They came within barely a hundred yards from the top, but had to turn back in a raging storm and never got a second chance at the summit. The first ascent was accomplished just the following year by a party led by Hudson Stuck. In a way, Brownie was completing unfinished family business by climbing McKinley with us.

The next few days were spent doing miscellaneous jobs: typing lists of supplies, roping bundles to be airdropped to us, packing parachute containers, buying cornmeal. One day we went out to Lake Spenard to watch a load of our stuff being flown out to the Muldrow Glacier. Mount McKinley looked like a pink iceberg on the horizon.

Just before leaving for the mountain, we were driving to Lake Spenard when we happened upon the site of an airplane accident. The plane had crashed into the nearby woods, and the pilot was being given blood plasma. A woman aboard had been killed. This scene made me very apprehensive. I was constantly reminding myself I had to get home safely to the children.

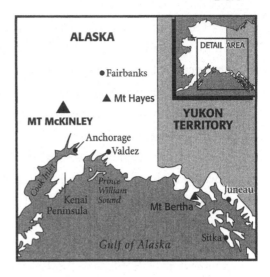

It was just about time to go. We settled problems of publicity and finances, and we found a deep-freeze plant that sold us frozen hamburger patties. Most fun of all, Brad and I bought candy bunnies to send to the children for Easter. All preparations completed, we were ready to tackle Mount McKinley.

Brownie and Shorty flew to the Muldrow Glacier to establish our base camp. It was a beautiful day, and they were beside themselves with excitement. It was especially meaningful for Brownie, remembering how close his father had come to reaching the summit that time long ago. Three days later, the two cameramen and Bill Hackett joined them.

Brad and I remained in Anchorage to take care of last-minute business. We consulted with the park superintendent's office on allowing our radio operator, Red Solberg, to work from park headquarters. He was our contact with the outside world, scheduled to relay our stories to the newspapers from our camps on the mountain. We also had to arrange for our sled dogs to be sent by train from Anchorage to McKinley Park Station.

We hadn't even started on the mountain, but I was already more worried than I had been on Mount Bertha or Mount Hayes. On Bertha especially, I was more carefree. I didn't have any children then. The whole atmosphere surrounding the McKinley trip was exciting and adventurous—but it was also more scary.

Our pilot, Haakon Christensen ("Chris" to us), was going to take Brad up for a photographic flight, along with Augie Hiebert, a friend who was an executive at a local radio station. I accepted an invitation to go along—a bit apprehensive because I knew we would fly to an altitude of at least 16,000 feet in order for Brad to get his pictures, and the plane provided no supplementary oxygen.

As we ascended, the awesome mass of Mount McKinley came into view. It was like a huge birthday cake covered with marshmallow frosting. As we flew higher and higher, Augie and I suddenly began giggling—apparently from the lack of oxygen. We started to feel somewhat disconnected from events as the plane circled and Brad took pictures. The door had been removed from the plane so Brad could lean out and shoot. Augie and I were freezing. Lacking enough oxygen and shivering from the cold, I had to wonder how I would function on the mountain.

At last, on April 9, with all business details attended to, Brad and I landed at the 5,700-foot base camp on the Muldrow Glacier at McGonagall Pass. When we landed, our two filmmakers had their cameras grinding away. I was so nervous and excited I suddenly felt the need to relieve myself. But where to go, in privacy, on a glacier? No trees, of course. And because of crevasses, you can't just wander around looking for a spot. I found a small snowdrift near the tent and hid behind it for a moment.

We had a delicious dinner that evening of beef and gravy, dehydrated potatoes and frozen peas, topped off with frozen strawberries. Frozen foods were to make our experience much more comfortable. The Birdseye Company had given us a huge supply.

The temperature was 12 degrees Fahrenheit before we all settled into our tents. Overnight it dropped to 30 below zero. I was restless that night, from a combination of cold and altitude. We may not have been very high on McKinley, but still we were more than a mile high in altitude. I knew I would eventually acclimatize, but I was praying the cold wouldn't last.

The next day we were busy testing the stoves, experimenting with our radio, and straightening out our supplies. It snowed all afternoon, so we huddled in the cook tent. A treat of frozen peaches with our supper helped keep up morale. Over the next few days, blessed with gorgeous weather, we took care of more chores. We bagged sugar and dehydrated potatoes, with one day's supply in each bag. We collected loads of supplies dropped to us by parachute or by free fall from a C-47. On the afternoon of April 12, the Emergency Rescue Squadron's C-45 arrived from Anchorage carrying Jim Gale, scientist Hugo Victoreen, and Len Shannon, a reporter assigned to us by International News Serice (INS). We all walked up the hill behind camp to watch the sunset glow on McKinley.

The next day we had a little unexpected excitement. Jim Gale walked up-glacier to mark the trail with willow wands to help us find our way back to camp in case of whiteout conditions. He was accompanied by two other members of our expedition—Bob Craig, a climber from Seattle who was in his early twenties, and Grant Pearson, a former McKinley Park superintendent who had previously climbed the mountain and at age fifty was back to try it again. They returned to camp with quite a story. They had not been closely attending to the rope, and Bob fell forty-five feet into a snow-covered crevasse. They were able to extricate him without serious injury, but it shook everyone up. At dinner, Grant reiterated Brad's earlier lectures on the danger of crevasses and reminded us that on this particular glacier they were anywhere and everywhere.

Three days later, musher Earl Norris made a dramatic entrance into camp, shouting "Gee" and "Haw" to direct his nine huskies over the rocks behind our tents. He was exhausted after the seventy-mile journey from park headquarters. Friends of Brad's had recommended Earl as just the man to handle the dogs that would be used to ferry supplies on the glacier.

On a day when Brad and several others were out breaking trail after a snow-storm, I got up to handle the 8:30 radio schedule. I lit the big Coleman firepot inside the tent to start breakfast, but to my horror it erupted into flames. I yelled "Help, fire!" But it came out in a feeble voice. My second yell was more frantic. I kicked the firepot out the tent door, then grabbed Earl's heavy wool shirt that was hanging on a line at the roof of the tent and used it to smother the burning gasoline. I was still shaking when two faces appeared at the tent door. It was the RKO photographers, Bill Deeke and George Wellsted.

"Did you call for help?" they asked.

"I sure did," I shouted. "The tent was going up in flames!"

They explained apologetically that they were slow to respond because they couldn't get their sleeping bags unzipped.

When we realized nothing terribly serious had happened, we tried to figure out why the firepot had burst into flames. We guessed that someone had turned the fuel valve incorrectly and that gas had trickled out over the tent floor all night. So it was ready to explode when I put the match to the stove. From that day on we always checked the valve before going to bed, and the disaster was never repeated. And Earl never held it against me that I'd singed his heavy, warm shirt.

The next week was filled with varied tasks: trips up-glacier to establish Camp 2 at 7,400 feet, sessions of surveying as part of Brad's work to map Mount McKinley, and orgies of photography. All the time these basic activities were going on, reporter Len Shannon was sending out stories that we all thought sounded outrageously dramatic. And we told him so in no uncertain terms.

Shannon had a different perspective from ours.

"Your activities may seem routine to you," he told us, "but to the public and to me they are as dramatic as going to the moon."

He was probably right. We tended to forget that not many people had experience climbing on mountains in Alaska. It may have been the norm for us, but it was pretty dramatic stuff for much of the public. The average person hasn't experienced high altitude, extreme cold weather, snowstorms, and spectacular views from high in the mountains. But the members of the expedition were modest and understated people as a rule, so we were uncomfortable with all the drama Shannon put into his stories.

We sensed that Shannon was unhappy on the mountain. Still, we were surprised when our pilot, Chris, flew in to pick him up one day. Apparently he had sent out a secret SOS, begging to be rescued from our dangerous adventures. The poor fellow, we learned later, hated to fly, hated life on the glacier, and hated the cold. His parting words to us were, "When I get back to Los Angeles, I'm going into the darkest nightclub I can find, smoke a big, black cigar, and never look at snow again."

The pilot returned four days later with Bill Sterling, another reporter for INS, who quickly adjusted to life on the glacier and wrote some interesting stories. He became the third Bill in our group, after Bill Deeke and Bill Hackett.

On April 26, Brad, Bill Deeke, George Wellsted, and I hiked up to Camp 2. The last hill into camp seemed interminable. Exhaustion forced George and Bill to leave their packs below camp. They had never backpacked like this before.

I cooked supper while the rest of the gang descended the hill to help Earl with the dogs and to pick up the abandoned packs. All thirteen of us had supper in a five-man pyramid-shaped tent. What a squeeze that was. We were beginning to feel like one big family—a particularly close family. When Brad and I retired to our own tent, we had another crisis with our little Coleman stove, nearly setting the tent on fire. The next day—April 27, 1947—was the seventh anniversary of our wedding

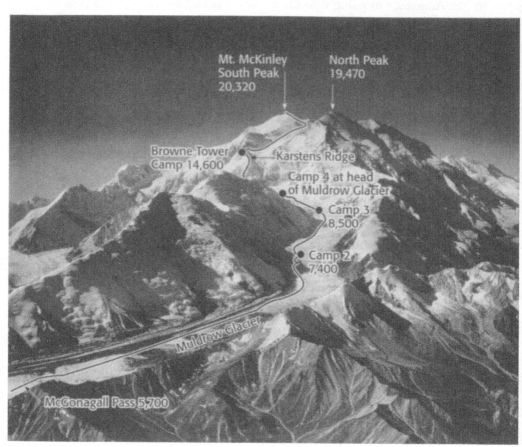

Mt. McKinley
South Peak
20,320

North Peak
19,470

Browne Tower
Camp 14,600

Karstens Ridge

Camp 4 at head
of Muldrow Glacier

Camp 3
8,500

Camp 2
7,400

Muldrow Glacier

McGonagall Pass 5,700

We established four camps up the Muldrow Glacier, from McGonagall Pass up to the head of the glacier, before moving up Karstens Ridge to the upper part of the route.

CHAPTER *Eleven*
TO HIGH CAMP

BROWNIE, JIM GALE, AND BILL HACKETT moved up to the site of Camp 3 in the middle of the big Muldrow icefall at 8,500 feet. The rest of us took light loads up to a cache at 7,700 feet. We looked like worker ants as we wound our way through the huge crevasses.

Earl Norris and his dogs succeeded in bringing all our supplies up from Base Camp. Work done, we were tired and hungry as we settled down to a quiet evening, the temperature at 5 degrees. Bob Craig cut Hugo's hair. Brad and Sterling worked on a story to be released to the press—part of the bargain we had made to help interest the public in mountaineering.

The next day cleared beautifully. As we were relaying more loads up to the cache, we heard the Emergency Rescue Squadron plane making continual passes far above us, apparently dropping loads of supplies for us to use higher on the mountain. Brad immediately got on the radio to ask the pilot to hold off on the operation until we could get someone on the ground at the airdrop site. The snow up there might easily be soft and deep and we were afraid the bundles might get buried before we could find them. We needed to be able to see exactly where they hit.

After a lunch of macaroni and cheese at Camp 2, Brad, Grant, and I took a load of supplies up to the 7,700-foot cache. On the way back down, my snowshoes slipped on an icy sidehill and I was quickly headed for a huge crevasse. Brad and Grant were able to hold me on the rope between them. Then I crawled on my hands and knees back onto the route.

I was awakened May 1 by a song for Shorty on his nineteenth birthday. It snowed gently all day. Hugo and Bob came up to Camp 2 and the rest of us carried a load to the cache, traveling through a maze of crevasses and over thin bridges of snow. By May 3 we had established Camp 3 at 8,500 feet. We built two igloos halfway up the big icefall. Jim Gale had learned how to build igloos from Eskimos during the war, and we found they were much more comfortable than tents. They don't flap when the wind is blowing, and in a blizzard, you don't have to keep digging them out.

Shorty, Brad, and I began trying to establish a trail to a rock ledge on the side of the glacier in order to make glacier-motion studies. We tried to traverse a steep snow slope, but gave up at first because we feared the loose snow would let go and send us down into the crevasses below. Brad and Shorty later got to the ledge, and our study showed us that the glacier (and all of us with it) were moving downhill at a rate of six inches a day.

We woke to a lovely, clear morning on May 7. At 9:00 a.m. Brad, Jim, and I headed up to 11,000 feet to prepare for a supply drop from the plane. At first the route was slippery and steep, but the second half up to 11,000 feet was a gradual climb and very pleasant.

We waited and waited, but no plane appeared, so we helped Jim and Hugo set up a new camp—Camp 4—at 11,000 feet at the very head of the Muldrow Glacier, and they decided to stay up there. The mountain became socked in, and just as we were ready to start back down to Camp 3, we heard the roar of the plane. It made several runs overhead, then on the fourth run the pilot radioed that the air was too turbulent and he couldn't make the drop. The plane made the drop about 4:30 the next afternoon. We all got piles of mail and had fun reading it.

On May 10, I tied into a rope with Brownie and Bob Craig and set off from Camp 3, very relieved that this would be my last trip for a while up those slippery sidehills in the icefall.

Courtesy of the National Geographic Society

Our route up Karstens Ridge took us to the Browne Tower Camp at 14,600 feet, where Bill Hackett, Hugo Victoreen, and I were trapped by a nine-day blizzard. When the weather finally cleared, we continued up Harper Glacier to our highest camp, at Denali Pass.

It was strange. One minute on McKinley you can be in a whiteout, freezing with the wind blasting you in the face, and later the same day the sun can be shining out of a cloudless sky. We didn't have sunscreen in those days, but I always wore a white hat, dark glasses, and a handkerchief covering my mouth on sunny days. We all had sunburned lips most of the time.

When we arrived at the site of Camp 4, I was overwhelmed by the magnificence of the place. You could look 4,000 feet up Karstens Ridge toward Browne Tower, and you could watch huge avalanches crash down off Harper

Glacier. We were in the presence of McKinley history: Karstens Ridge and Harper Glacier were named for two members of the first party to reach the summit, back in 1913, Harry Karstens and Walter Harper. Browne Tower was named for Brownie's father, Belmore Browne.

We made sure our camp was a safe distance from the end of the powerful Harper Glacier, but I remember how exciting it was to hear its loud rumblings during the night. At first the noise kept me awake, but soon I became accustomed to it—even found it rather comforting.

I spent the rest of the day melting snow for water and preparing dinner for those climbing up after us. Brad and Grant didn't arrive until late afternoon. The next morning we went up Karstens Ridge to put in a fixed rope on a particularly steep pitch, doing the job in dense fog and blowing snow. Back at Camp 4 we set to work establishing a really comfortable place for members of the party who wouldn't be going to the summit. We rigged up the nine-by-twelve cook tent with seats along the sides and a long table in the middle. We had plenty of boxes to work with from the stuff that had been dropped by parachute.

That evening, flush with the success of all our progress, we sat around our new dining table, quite relaxed. Soon the boys were telling jokes and their language became a little bawdy. Suddenly, Grant, the senior member of our group, held up his hand and shouted to the assembled gang: "Stop that language! We have a lady in our midst and I won't have you using that kind of language in front of her!"

It was really very amusing. He was an old-fashioned guy and he was banging on the table. I was laughing inwardly because by then I knew perfectly well how to cuss. I thanked Grant for being so considerate. The men always treated me like a lady anyway, but after that outburst I don't remember ever hearing them swear again.

Later that evening we contacted McKinley Park headquarters by radio and serenaded Grant's wife and daughter, Shirley and Margaret. Not to be outdone, they responded with a rendition of "I've Been Working on the Railroad." The next day was Mother's Day. Since I couldn't spend the day with my children back home in Massachusetts, I went for a long walk—up to 12,000 feet on Mount McKinley.

The move up to the next high camp was now set to begin. To establish a camp at Browne Tower at 14,600 feet was going to be a fairly difficult task. Part of the work involved packing heavy movie equipment up Karstens Ridge. Our first project was to build an igloo on a short, level spot at 12,000 feet where climbers could rest on the trip up the steep ridge.

Brad and I spent the night in the igloo. We made a delicious supper of vegetable soup, chicken á la king, and potatoes, and a scrumptious dessert of fig pudding with orange sauce (the secret ingredients included sugar mixed with Tang). During the night we couldn't make the igloo warm enough to be really comfortable. The ceiling kept dripping on us. In the morning we were visited by a little junco, who appeared to enjoy our company. We were surprised to find a bird at this altitude. He must have been blown off-course by the wind.

Brad and Bob Craig, the first members of our team to reach Browne Tower, had a wonderful surprise. They found a cache left by the party on the 1932 climb of McKinley, only the second ascent of the mountain. Despite all the snowfall in the previous fifteen years, the long pole marking the cache was still visible. In the cache were powdered soups, soap, and crackers—all items useful to us. They were still good, unspoiled. Grant, who was still down at Camp 4, got a kick out of the news because he had been a member of that expedition.

It is interesting to note that after Mount McKinley was first success-fully climbed in 1913 by Hudson Stuck's party, almost no one went there to climb. Nearly twenty years passed until there was another ascent. Quite a contrast with today when a thousand people a year try to climb McKinley. The first climbers were true explorers. The climbers today are on vacation!

My climb up Karstens Ridge was not as difficult as I had expected. Brad cut good steps, although they were always quite a stretch for my short legs. In the one bad spot, a fixed rope was firmly attached. It was unnerving to look down 4,000 feet to the Traleika Glacier below. I found I had to concentrate on the climbing, keeping my eyes on the ridge, not on the glacier.

Soon there were five of us at the rather precarious but magnificent campsite at 14,600 feet—Hugo, Bill Hackett, Brad, Jim, and myself. I woke up in the morning with a splitting headache and nausea. I could only get down a little bit of grapefruit and tea, which I promptly lost. Guess I had a touch of altitude sickness. I slept all morning, took two aspirin, and by afternoon felt better. We got some more mail, brought up to us from our camp at the head of the Muldrow Glacier, where it had been airdropped. This special delivery mail had all sorts of good news about how well the children were doing and some cute drawings they made for us. I missed them so.

CHAPTER 12 *Twelve*

THE BLIZZARD

BRAD AND JIM NOW PUSHED ON ALONE, heading toward the 18,000-foot level. They were the most experienced and wanted to establish camp in Denali Pass before the rest of us joined them. It was said of Denali Pass that the wind stopped blowing there only long enough to change direction. They set off to do the hard work, and we planned to join them in a couple of days.

A long and violent storm intervened, and we were not able to join them until long after we were expected. We were stuck. A raging nine-day blizzard pinned me, Hugo, and Bill at the high camp at 14,600 feet, and caught Brad and Jim higher up on the mountain. There was nothing to do but hunker down and ride it out.

On the first night of the storm, Brad radioed that he and Jim were in an emergency igloo at 15,500 feet. He was about to take a sleeping pill and he advised me to do the same. In stormy conditions, even if you are safely protected from the elements, the noise can keep you from sleeping.

At first we felt the storm wouldn't last long. We were wrong. After the first two days we established a routine for daily life. It helped prevent us from going crazy. We had our three sleeping bags laid out on the floor of the igloo that Brad and Jim had built before they left. We slept there but did all of our cooking in the nearby tent. Because the high altitude made our movements sluggish and because of the cramped quarters in the tent, we found that it took all morning to get breakfast made and eaten and to wash the dishes. We then would make radio contact with Brad and Jim above us and with the climbers at Camp 4 below us. By then it would be lunchtime.

All we could do during this endless storm was wait. We talked or read. We had some *Reader's Digests* that we passed around, and in the afternoons we studied those magazines like textbooks. It was easy to get on each other's nerves in a situation like that. I didn't have much in common with these fellows. Bill was in the Army and Hugo was a physicist. We discussed the stories in the magazines. We talked about all sorts of subjects, some of them political, and we didn't always agree. On interracial marriage, for instance. Hugo was married to a black woman, and Bill was not in favor. I chose to offer Bill a short lecture on tolerance.

Sometimes we played the spelling game called Ghost. We often had heated arguments about the correct spelling of a word. I usually stopped the disputes by saying we should check with Brad during our morning radio hookup. We considered him a walking dictionary.

Hugo, Bill, and I worried about being blown away when we went outside to relieve ourselves. The snow was driven through your clothing, and the wind took your breath away. Hugo finally just used a tin can, but that didn't help me. When I ventured forth during one brief lull in the wind, Hugo and Bill kept shouting after me, "Are you OK?"

The weather was so violent that when we left the cook tent after dinner to make our way back to the igloo, we held each other's hands. The distance was only twenty-five feet, but we needed to hold to each other for safety. Someone might wander off into the storm or be swept off the ridge by a gust of wind. It seemed like a long distance between our two temporary structures, and we faced a deadly fall on both sides of us. It was a long way down to the Muldrow Glacier.

The storm went on and on. My diary entries became very repetitive: "A terrible day."

Then, "Another terrible day."

Then, "Worst day yet."

One day I radioed Sterling with information for a story on me to use in his daily dispatch to the International News Service. Now the truth was much better than fiction, and it wasn't hard to make the story sound dramatic.

On the seventh day of the storm, I wrote in my diary: "Our courage is beginning to wane. Another horrible day of high winds and blowing snow."

We received word by radio from Camp 4 that two tents had been rendered useless by the storm when the poles went through the tent peaks and ripped them. Brad reported from 18,000 feet that it had snowed another foot that night and that he and Jim were running out of gas and food. It was shaping up as a critical situation. We managed to stay calm and patient, though, and on May 29, after nine days, the storm abated. It took me a while to truly believe the wind had died down. The worst of the storm was over.

Hugo and Bill trekked down the ridge to Camp 4 and brought back two gallons of gas, some cereal, fruit, and powdered milk. With the storm blowing out and the sky clear and sunny on May 30, we now hoped we would be receiving some fresh goods via airdrop. However, after making one drop at 18,000 feet, the plane retreated. Too windy. The crew then tried a drop at 11,000 feet, but there were too many clouds.

They knew we were running low on critical supplies, so they kept trying. Finally they completed the drops at 18,000 feet, up where Brad and Jim were, but some bundles were never found, including one that included mail for me and Brad. We understood how tough it would be to hit an airdrop target at this altitude, trying to zero in on the high camp between the two peaks of Mount McKinley. We were extremely grateful to get what we could.

It was now time for Hugo, Bill, and me to move three miles and 3,600 feet in elevation up to Denali Pass to join Brad and Jim. We had been cooped up in a small igloo and a tent for almost two weeks. Our muscles were stiff and we were not in very good shape. Our diet of C-rations was less than

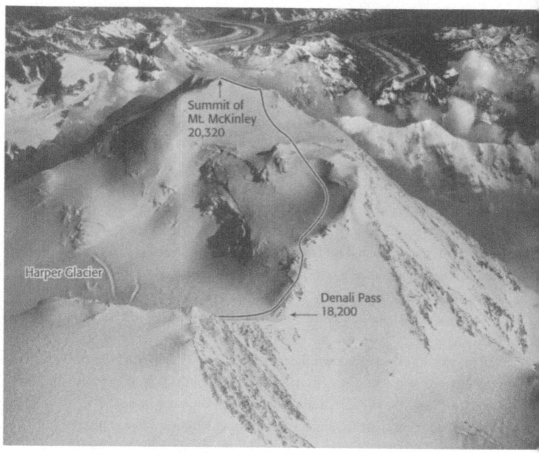

Courtesy of the National Geographic Society

On June 6, 1947, I left from high camp at Denali Pass with Brad and the others in our team and headed toward our final goal, the highest point in North America.

inspiring and our appetites had shrunk. In this condition we were about to set off for Denali Pass and, from there, the summit of McKinley.

Brad had asked us to bring up a few things from Camp 4. He would radio down and ask us not to forget to bring this, that, and the other—things like sugar, or maybe an extra pair of crampons. Complying with his requests made our packs heavier than we wished, but we had to try. My average carrying weight was thirty-five pounds, and adding more weight threw me off-balance. I soon paid a price for my helpfulness.

Brad told us to be certain to wear crampons on the steep route up to Denali Pass. But Bill and Hugo didn't want to wear them so I didn't put mine on either. This was the wrong decision, but maybe we just weren't thinking so well after sitting around at high altitude for so long, doing nothing. I wore felt boots, which could not dig into the slick surface. Bill was leading, but the steps he kicked weren't that good, so I was working just as hard behind him. Hugo followed behind me, third on the rope.

We were crossing a very slippery side-slope just above camp when suddenly my awkward pack shifted to one side. I lost my balance, and before I knew what happened, I was sliding toward Harper Glacier far below. I slid only about a dozen feet before the rope pulled tight and stopped me. My light weight helped us all: Bill and Hugo were not prepared for my fall and I might easily have yanked them off their feet and dragged us all down, but they pulled the rope taut and were able to stop me.

As soon as I recovered from the shock of the slide I yelled to Bill to give my crampons to me. I was very shaken up. It took a huge amount of effort and willpower to climb back up the slope to Bill and Hugo. I tried to be a good sport about it, to act as if nothing had happened. But I was shattered—not only frightened, but exhausted.

This was the key moment in the worst day of my life. Suddenly I burst into tears. Bill looked down at me, very sympathetically, and said, "Why did you come on this trip, Barbara?" Still sobbing, I murmured, "Because Brad wanted me to, and I wanted to be with him." Bill was undone by the tears. A boy never knows what to do when a girl cries.

After a brief rest we all calmed down. The boys gallantly took a few items from my pack and added them to their loads. We started off again. It was excruciatingly hot crossing the 15,000-foot plateau of Harper Glacier, but we finally reached 15,500 feet and the igloo that Brad and Jim had built on their way to Denali Pass before the storm struck.

We had a lunch of chocolate and raisins, but neither of those usually tasty foods was appetizing at this altitude. My strength was waning, but we struggled on and came to another cache left by Brad and Jim at 17,000 feet.

It was a bitter fight for me to continue higher. Here we sat down to gather strength, and I noticed that Bill and Hugo seemed to relish the rest as much as I did. I got a second wind and could now move slowly, but steadily.

The last half mile to Denali Pass was exhausting for all three of us. Bill was leading, and luckily for me he needed to stop for breath every few steps, so I was able to follow without calling out for rests. As the lone female, the last thing I wanted to display was anything that might be considered a woman's frailty, even though my back and ribs were aching from my fall earlier in the day. It was bad enough that I had cried after I slid down the slope. I wanted to keep proving that my presence wasn't a hindrance, but that day stretched my limits.

Suddenly in the distance I saw a tiny, black speck. I imagined it might be Brad coming to help me. The tiny speck turned out to be a tent. As we came over the final rise, I spotted on the horizon what looked like Brad coming toward us. When I realized it really was him, an extra spurt of energy propelled me into his arms, and with tears rolling down my cheeks, I whispered, "Thank God you're here."

After a very light supper, all five of us crawled into our sleeping bags in a large Army wall tent. I did not sleep well and woke up in the morning with the usual altitude sickness of nausea and headache. I attributed part of my problem to sleeping with my head inside the bag; maybe I wasn't getting enough air. I also wondered if the sleeping pills were contributing to the headache. I took two aspirin and felt pretty good the rest of the day.

Our supply plane flew over at 3:30 p.m., dropping four parachute items and eighteen free-fall items. Everything landed three-quarters of a mile down the glacier. Luckily, Brad and Jim, who were now thoroughly acclimatized to 18,000 feet, were able to find everything. Still, it was a huge job to lug the stuff back up to camp.

We needed these supplies. Unlike modern expeditions where the climbers carry everything in their packs and operate under strict time limits, we planned our expedition to be repeatedly resupplied. We had a large group of people, we were also conducting scientific work, and we were going to be on the mountain for an unknown amount of time. With these supplies, we didn't have to rush to the top. We had time. We didn't have to try to go for the summit on a bad day. If it was stormy, we could stay put indefinitely. That was our advantage.

Standing at 18,400 feet on Mount McKinley, I took in the view to the northwest.

CHAPTER 13 *Thirteen*

ON THE ROOF OF NORTH AMERICA

LIFE AT THIS HIGH CAMP WAS NOT COMFORTABLE. We took sleeping pills, but they did not prevent my dry, hacking cough from continuing, or my frequent bouts of gasping for breath in the middle of the night. The wind was almost always blowing and the temperature stayed well below zero. We tried to make our bed more comfortable, putting parachutes and cardboard from cartons under our sleeping bags. At one point Brad gave me a pep talk, telling me: "Don't get discouraged, you'll feel much better as you acclimatize." A more-or-less continuous headache was my biggest problem. I felt that if I could only get rid of that, I would be of some use. It was now June 1. In an attempt to bolster my morale, I spent time picturing the children playing in their sunsuits in our yard back home.

After a few days in this camp, life seemed brighter. My headache disappeared. Shorty and Bob arrived on June 2, and they dragged into camp looking just as exhausted as we had felt a few days earlier. The next day, Bill Deeke, Brownie, Grant, and Bill Sterling staggered in. There was quite a crowd in camp, and we had a good time that evening over supper, hashing over all the things that happened while we were separated during the storm.

Before retiring to our tents, we all walked over to Denali Pass to look down on the West Buttress of Mount McKinley. At this moment Brad recognized the West Buttress as a safer route for approaching the summit. But we could

Roped up on the ridge above Denali Pass on Mount McKinley, I got a good look up at our route. The summit is still hidden above the dome of snow in the upper left.

not know then that four years later, Brad would lead the first ascent of the West Buttress, establishing a route that would become the most popular way for climbers thereafter to attempt McKinley.

Now that everyone who was going to try for the summit had arrived in high camp, we busied ourselves trying to make life comfortable while waiting for good weather. We received an airdrop that included ice cream in anticipation of Brad's upcoming birthday. But it arrived in liquid form, all mixed up with Quaker Oats.

June 6 dawned clear and windless. It looked like a good day for a summit climb. I was feeling better and was anticipating the climb to the top with more pleasure than apprehension.

We started out slowly. Brad assigned me to a rope with Bill Deeke, Grant, and Brownie. I actually found the going quite easy. I was well-acclimatized.

Courtesy of the National Geographic Society

Bill Hackett gets a cup of hot coffee with lots of sugar at 20,000 feet on Mount McKinley as I take care of the pouring. We had less than half an hour to go to reach the summit.

Only two hundred vertical feet of climbing remained to reach the summit of the tallest mountain in North America. Shorty Lange was in the lead, followed by me and Bill Hackett.

From high camp at 18,000 feet, we trekked upward to 19,300 feet—now only a thousand feet in elevation below the summit.

At that point, Grant decided to turn back. He was fifty years old, and he said he worried about the strain on his heart. He had promised his wife he would not do anything foolish. And of course Grant had already been to the summit, on the 1932 expedition.

After a brief rest and a snack of figs and orange juice, we switched ropes and I continued on, now roped with Brad, Shorty, and Bill Hackett. Jim Gale and Bob Craig were also making the climb that day. Brad chose the beginning of the summit ridge to unrope from us to take photographs. We were up so high that every step took extra effort and it was a tough push. But then I got a second wind and became sure I could make it to the top.

We kept moving steadily upward, the summit inching ever closer. And then, all of a sudden, we were there—standing on the roof of North America, at 20,320 feet above sea level, with a thrilling panorama of Alaska stretched out before us—almost 100,000 square miles in a single sweep.

On the summit, the wind was gusting to twenty or more miles an hour and the temperature was 20 below zero. I jumped up and down, trying to stay warm. We were on the summit for an hour, a very long time under those conditions. Climbers who make the summit often take a quick look at the view, snap a few pictures, and start their descent as soon as possible. But Brad was always involved in scientific work, so some things had to get done, and we all took turns helping him.

When Brad finished his surveying, his fingers totally numb from the cold, we started down on a rope together and the others followed. Going down was so much easier on the lungs. But the others beat us back to camp because Brad kept stopping to take pictures. I didn't mind at all. In fact I was glad, because every time he stopped to click the shutter I got extra rest.

It was now an easy trip for me. We were going slowly enough for me to savor the scene, with fluffy, snow-white clouds billowing up over the lowlands. The slower pace also gave me time to think about what we had accomplished. It was a victorious day for all of us, but especially for Brownie, whose father had come so close to being the first person to reach the

It was June 6, 1947, and Brad and I stood atop the roof of North America: the summit of Mount McKinley at 20,320 feet.

summit. I had just become the first woman to stand atop Mount McKinley, but the accomplishment didn't really mean that much to me at that moment, perhaps because it had not been a special goal of mine. But I knew Brad was proud of me for doing it and that made me feel good.

The next day, June 7, was Brad's thirty-seventh birthday. I should have known he would want to do something special. Just as I was settling down for a restful day of reading and letter writing, Brad opened the tent flap and shouted, "Let's climb the North Peak! We'll never get such a perfect day again!"

The North Peak? The South Peak of McKinley is the high point on the mountain and that is where everyone climbs. But Brad wasn't satisfied. The North Peak beckoned to him. He needed to survey from it to complete his map of McKinley. The North Peak is 19,470 feet high and is two miles north of the true summit. It would be like climbing McKinley all over again, only with a detour.

The idea caught me off guard. But I had felt good the day before, going for the summit. I wasn't that out of breath. I didn't gasp. So I felt I could do it again, even if that wouldn't have been my first choice. When Brad announced his plan, I thought I heard a few mild groans from inside the other tents, but a group of us rallied to our leader's call.

In a short while we were roped up and on our way. I tied in with Bob, Jim, and Bill Sterling, while Brad, Shorty, and Bill Hackett went ahead to set up the surveying instrument, the theodolite, and get started with the work that had to be done on the North Peak.

June 7 was indeed a marvelous day. This ascent turned out to be much more pleasant than the climb to the true summit because there was no wind, the air was crystal clear, and the view was cloudless as far as the eye could see. From the top we looked down the awesome Wickersham Wall onto Peters Glacier, a drop of more than 14,000 feet. While Brad carried out his surveying, the rest of us enjoyed the spectacular view and nibbled on crackers and dates.

Sterling and I roped up and started down ahead of the others, with me leading down the steep rock and snow cliff just opposite our camp. I was a climbing veteran compared with Sterling, a reporter with no previous mountaineering experience. I thought I was doing well as a leader, but he kept shouting at me to slow down.

So we ended up climbing both peaks of McKinley, one after the other, on consecutive days. We felt that would make the people at RKO happy. Once the climbing and surveying were finished, we had to write stories for the press. Our expedition was financed in order to bring attention to climbing and to the RKO movie, so we had that obligation. On June 8, Bill Deeke, Bob, Brad, and I went up the trail to the first rocks and did some filming.

For two days we worked on news stories, trying to make them dramatic enough for the press while at the same time not exaggerating our experiences. Before our climb, only fifteen people had reached the summit, no women among them, so we had to appreciate the fact that the press was going to make a big fuss about our accomplishments, no matter what. One radio station wanted a story immediately, so I dictated a report to our radio operator at Wonder Lake and he relayed it to Anchorage. My sister Edith learned the news as she was driving to her home in Florida. She heard on the radio that I had become the first woman to reach the summit of Mount McKinley.

We had now fulfilled our commitment to RKO by climbing the mountain and then writing all about it, so it was time to descend and get back safely to Anchorage and then to my children. On June 11, a clear but windy day, Bob, Bill Deeke, and I started down to our Browne Tower camp, the same place where I had spent those nine long days in the blizzard with Bill Hackett and Hugo Victoreen. By our lunch break Brad and Bill Hackett caught up to us. A quick look at the sky told us we should not rest for long. There were high winds over the South Peak and the weather was socking in fast.

Brad tied me on his rope and together the two of us started down Karstens Ridge. We were both carrying heavier loads than was advisable because we wanted to avoid making two trips over the ridge. Brad's pack weighed ninety pounds and he was also dragging a duffel bag beside him. He finally abandoned the duffel bag, which contained one of our sleeping bags, because it kept swinging in front of him and throwing him off balance. I was carrying forty pounds, the most I could manage.

The weather seemed more ominous by the minute and Brad urged me to hurry. At 12,000 feet, at the steepest point on the ridge, I had a terrible time finding the steps he had chopped on an icy spot on the way up. They were now covered with snow and were much too far apart for my short legs. I had to back down the steps. I was scared stiff going down a steep pitch of blue ice.

Once again he told me to hurry and I got very angry. I glared at Brad looking down at me from the crest of the ridge and yelled, "Goddamn the son of a bitch who cut these steps!"

Brad was surprised by my outburst and politely responded that he was the one who cut them. Whereupon I swiftly shouted back with great force, "That goes for you, too!"

I controlled my anger briefly while concentrating on the next step, but Brad jerked the rope and shouted to me, "You've simply got to move faster. The storm is approaching rapidly."

I looked at him, fifteen feet away, and said calmly, "I am the mother of three small children and I've got to get down from here safely."

He replied immediately, "Don't forget, I'm the father of those small children and I want to get down safely, too."

Once below that spot, the going was easier. I was still on the rope with Brad, but I no longer had to back down searching for good footholds because I could now make my own in the soft snow.

I saw three tiny black spots on the ridge below. As we kept descending, it became clear that three people were coming up the ridge. We were astonished because this was the first time in history anyone had met another climbing party on Mount McKinley. Brad immediately recognized the significance of the moment, and what leaped into his imagination was an image of that famous moment in history when Stanley met Livingstone in the wilds of the African jungle.

As we approached the climbers, Brad stuck out his hand and said, "Dr. Livingstone, I presume." He was demonstrating a great sense of the occasion and it was quite funny. Unfortunately the wit was lost on the leader of the other group, who replied, "No, my name is Morton Wood. I come from Seattle."

The three climbers quickly realized it would be easier for them if they made use of the extra food and fuel we had cached along the way and followed our established trail upward. As it turned out, they still weren't able to reach the summit. They returned a few years later and did reach the top, but it was on that trip that Elton Thayer was killed.

Finally Brad and I arrived back at Camp 4 at 11,000 feet, at the head of the Muldrow Glacier, where we found our dog driver, Earl Norris. What a wonderful feeling to be at an elevation low enough that I could breathe easily. And my coughing stopped. The others arrived back in Camp 4 later that evening. As we relished our comparative comfort in this relaxing camp, we felt sorry for Hugo, Jim, and Shorty, who were still up at 18,000 feet carrying out the cosmic ray work. They were scheduled to be there for another week.

Brad and I were looking forward to a heavenly sleep at this lower elevation, but we were short the one sleeping bag that was now reposing up higher in the snow in the abandoned duffel bag. We had to sleep head to foot in one bag and it wasn't very comfortable. But it was cozy.

Sunburned and happy, I relax at our camp at Cache Creek. We were only a few miles from a ranger station and the end of our McKinley expedition.

CHAPTER 14
Fourteen
MIXED EMOTIONS

WE WERE LUCKY TO BE LOWER on the mountain now because a fresh storm blew in and we were snowbound for three days. A blizzard piled up two feet of snow—a good, old-fashioned New England-style blizzard with howling winds. Early each morning Brad stuck his head out the tent door to judge our prospects for descending, but most of the time all he could see was a thick fog. Poor Earl was itchy to go home. He was in love with a girl in Anchorage and was anxious to get back to her.

Finally on June 15 we decided to make a run for it. At 3:00 a.m. the fog was still on the ground, but at 6:00 a.m. the sun came out and we saw we were between two layers of clouds. The snow was deep and the fog was thick in places, and we had to break trail for the dogs. At one point in the dense fog I couldn't tell if I was going uphill or down. Throwing a snowball into the snow ahead provides a clue because of the tiny shadow of the hole where the snowball hits. What helped us most of all was finding the old willow wands that marked the trail, proving how important it was to put in these markers on the way up.

After a slow trip, we hit our cache at 7,700 feet, where we settled down for the night. Brad and Earl left with the dog team at 2:00 the next morning—an early start to take advantage of the easier travel on the frozen trail compared with slogging through sun-softened snow. The rest of us followed later in the morning.

The day was perfect, and the views of the mountain were magnificent. I kept looking back at McKinley with mixed emotions—fear, anger, and respect. I say anger because it was such hard work to climb it and because it kept lashing back at us with storms. I was reminded of a story Brad told me about returning from the Army ascent of McKinley in 1942. He was walking across the tundra with Peter Webb, a Canadian who had made the summit but had not enjoyed the experience. They stopped for a rest and Brad was admiring the view. He said to Peter, "Turn around and look at the mountain. It is magnificent. I have never seen it so clear." Peter replied, "No, I must not. Don't you remember in the Bible what happened to Lot's wife? If I looked at it, I would turn into a pillar of ice!"

Spring had come to the lowlands while we were freezing in the heights. The lower peaks that once seemed to be covered with marshmallow frosting were now a dull, grayish-black, with only small patches of snow here and there. The crevasses in the glacier had widened, and turquoise blue water rushed below us as we leaped over them. Some were too wide to jump, so we zigzagged around them. The smell of spring was in the air and we were in a state of euphoria as we moved down the glacier toward base camp. There is something inexplicably joyous and exciting about moving from a world that is 100 percent white to a world of bright color and living things.

When we hit McGonagall Pass, we found Brad and Bob in their underwear, with bare feet. As we approached the tent, we spotted a small pool of water nearby and rushed toward it to soothe our tired feet. Then we had a buffet lunch of crackers and lemonade. The temperature was now 70 degrees, and the hillsides were covered with green moss and purple flowers. I felt alive again.

It had been necessary to experience the severe cold, the sleepless nights, and the other high-altitude discomforts in order to really appreciate the luxury of my usual daily life. At high altitude, living day after day above seas of clouds, one has a feeling of separation from the rest of the world. After a month above 10,000 feet, I was more than ready for this return to the world below. Only one thing disrupted my feeling of euphoria—mosquitoes! They were bigger than ours at home, and slow to bite, but they formed such clouds around you that you felt almost suffocated. They could drive you mad.

The next morning Earl left with his dogs to haul the final load off the glacier. I knew how much I would miss the dogs. For me they were like children, and to give each one a loving pat was very comforting to me.

The boys began to relay loads down the rocky canyon below the glacier while the two cameramen and I arranged a cache of our leftovers to remain at McGonagall Pass. When Brad returned from his last relay down the canyon, he suggested that we abandon camp immediately and take advantage of the opportunity to travel in the coolness of the evening. At 11:00 p.m. we put together a meal of oatmeal and bacon, and with some feelings of sadness at leaving this beautiful spot, we headed down the soft, grassy slopes toward the McKinley River. After eight miles we were exhausted, so we set up a tent at Cache Creek. But with mosquitoes in the tent and the heat from the sun because there was no darkness this time of year, I got very little sleep.

The next morning, while we were again cooking oatmeal and bacon, we heard a tinkling of bells. There outside the tent stood Carl Anderson, a horsepacker, with three of his animals. Brad had radioed Carl to help us get our stuff out to Wonder Lake. Carl let me ride one of the horses as far as the McKinley River, where we took turns riding across the rushing, frigid waters, high from snowmelt in the mountains.

Once across the river, I walked the last four miles to the Wonder Lake ranger cabin. The two cameramen, Bill Deeke and George Wellsted, were so tired they rode the horses. They were not accustomed to this type of adventure, but they had been good companions throughout the trip. They also made a very good movie. *Operation White Tower* was later shown in theaters throughout the country.

On this day, June 20, 1947, I wrote in my diary: "Things are happening too fast for me!"

We had just trekked off the mountain after two and a half months of climbing and we were immediately thrown into the middle of frantic activity. Augie Hiebert wanted to interview us at his Fairbanks radio station, so we took the bus to McKinley Park headquarters, a distance of about ninety miles, and flew to Fairbanks. We did our radio interview with Augie the next morning. We saw General Hank Everest at Ladd Field and offered him thanks for the Army's air support of our expedition. Then we were flown back to McKinley Park in time for supper. In the midst of all this, we did not forget that June 21 was Betsy's first birthday. We would celebrate this big day in the life of our youngest daughter as soon as we got home.

We could not leave Alaska until Hugo, Jim, and Shorty, who were still doing the scientific work at 18,000 feet, were safely off the mountain. While waiting for their return, the rest of us had a wonderful time taking pictures of animals, fishing in Moose Creek, chatting with tourists, and generally getting used to being back in civilization again. We kept in radio contact with the men on the mountain and knew they should be approaching the McKinley River by June 30.

Sure enough, that morning from the road we spotted three tiny figures crossing the river. When they reached the road we picked them up in our truck. They were in amazingly good shape after such a long stay at high altitude. They did lose some weight, but were content with the success of their cosmic ray experiments. A little rest and good food put them back in top form.

One of our interesting experiences before leaving Alaska was a visit to the home of Johnny Busia, a miner who lived in Kantishna, an abandoned mining town near the end of the McKinley Park Highway. The gold rush was over, and now he and Bill Julian were the only inhabitants of Kantishna. They each lived in a cabin on opposite sides of the creek. The distance between their places was not great, but they were not on speaking terms. We never did find out why.

Johnny was famous for a kind of brew he kept stored in his cellar. When visitors appeared, the first thing he did was lift a trap door, disappear down the stairs, and return with mugs of a dark-colored liquid. He was very proud of the concoction. I took one careful sip and told Johnny how delicious it was. The truth was it had a horrible taste. Fortunately Johnny was interested in flowers and kept large plants in different corners of the room. While Brad engaged Johnny in conversation, I watered the plants with my grog.

There is quite a story about Bill Julian's death. Apparently, each morning in the winter, Johnny and Bill looked toward each other's cabin to see if smoke was coming out of the chimney. If it was, they went on ignoring each other. One morning Johnny didn't see any smoke at Bill's, so he crossed the creek and walked up to Bill's cabin. There he found him, dead and frozen stiff. It was winter, and the ground was frozen and impenetrable. Johnny explained to Brad what he did with Bill's body: "I just rolled him up in a tarp and stood him up in the woodshed until spring."

On July 2 we started on our way back to Massachusetts with a train ride from McKinley Park to Anchorage. Along the way we stopped at Curry to take the five-mile walk up to Curry Lookout for one last look at Mount McKinley. We headed up the trail at 1:00 a.m., still in daylight, for the beautiful walk through woods and high benches of tundra. We were worn out and sleepy by the time we reboarded the train, but it was worth the effort to say another farewell to the mountain that now meant so much to me.

In Anchorage we waited for the weather to clear for a final photographic flight around McKinley. On July 9, Brad went up with our pilot, Chris, in a four-hour flight. For the first time, Brad was able to pick out the exact spot where Belmore Browne had to turn back on his summit try. Our 18,000-foot camp was visible, as was the cosmic ray hut, surrounded by a deep hole where the wind whirled around it.

Brad and I flew out of Anchorage on July 10 and stopped in Minneapolis. We were rushed to death there with radio and newspaper interviews, luncheons and dinners. I still couldn't understand what all the fuss was about. Reporters expected me to come up with some deep psychological reason why I needed to be the first woman on the summit of Mount McKinley—why I felt I had to excel like this. They were always disappointed when I said I simply wanted to be with my husband. I explained that when I was first asked to join the expedition, I didn't want to go because I had three small children. I told them that when I finally was persuaded to go, I went with the knowledge that I could always turn back if I thought it was too dangerous. That simple information seemed to satisfy the reporters.

Today I'm smart enough to know I was doing something special. But at the time, my Aunt Cora said to me: "Barbara, you're never going to get swell-headed." I guess I was just brought up in a family where you didn't brag. I had no notion of being a role model for anyone, but I guess that's the way it has turned out. Years later, when the Boston Smith Club asked me to give a talk, I asked what they wanted me to talk about. They said, "Just your life."

On the last lap of our trip home, Brad and I grew more excited at the thought of seeing the children. We were met at the airport by friends, relatives, and newspaper reporters, but the only thing I wanted to do was get to our house. As we approached the front steps, my heart began to pound, and when the door opened and I heard the shrieks of joy from the children, I simply couldn't hold back the tears.

Dotty and Teddy grabbed us by the hand and dragged us to see the model of Mount McKinley they had built out of a pile of books covered with a snow-white sheet. Betsy was in a playpen nearby and perhaps wondered why these two people were hugging her so tight. She was just beginning to say her first words and it did not take her long to start calling us Mummy and Daddy. When I tucked each of the children into bed that night, I said a brief prayer of thanks that we were both home safely.

A family portrait from about 1949: Brad and I with our son, Teddy, and daughters Dotty (center) and Betsy.

CHAPTER 15 Fifteen

A NIGHT ON TOP

PEOPLE IN BOSTON DIDN'T KNOW MUCH about Mount McKinley in the 1940s, and they weren't much interested in it, either. But the first woman to do something unusual is bound to cause a bit of a stir. I finally realized that the attention was going to be focused on me for a while when our mayor, James Michael Curley, presented Brad and me with the key to the city.

The following year Brad was asked by *Life* magazine to organize a flight over West China to determine the height of Amni Machin. Pilots had flown near the peak several times during the war, and they brought back reports that it might be higher than Mount Everest. *Life* wanted to settle the question. Milton Reynolds, the ball-point pen king, financed the trip. Brad assembled a group of scientists and they set off in April, with plans to be gone a month. It stretched out to three.

With Brad gone much longer than expected, I found myself enlisted to fulfill some of his lecture commitments. For me, speaking before an audience was more frightening than climbing Mount McKinley. The first lecture was at the Cranbrook Institute in Michigan, which meant leaving the children for a couple of days with their grandparents. With great apprehension I flew to Detroit, two rolls of sixteen-millimeter film under my arm, and with no script except what I could remember from some of Brad's talks.

Word got around that I was going to give the lecture instead of Brad and so many people signed up to attend that the event was moved from a lecture hall to the gymnasium. I will never forget how lonely I felt standing on that huge stage and looking out over a vast sea of faces. I couldn't see an empty seat. I took a deep breath and explained why I was there instead of Brad, and then gave a short explanation of how the expedition came about. When I gave the signal for the film to start rolling, my heart nearly stopped beating. The film hadn't been rewound. Then I remembered what Brad told me he did when projection problems delayed a program.

"When things go wrong, just keep talking," he had said. It was good advice. I probably told the spectators more than they wanted to know about our expedition, but they seemed to be listening and I gained confidence. When it was over, many people told me how much they enjoyed the talk. After that it was much easier for me to carry out Brad's lecture commitments.

When Brad returned from China I learned that his trip had not been a howling success. Milton Reynolds and his pilot had abandoned the scientists in Peking (as Beijing was known then) because Reynolds was impatient about how long it took to get permits for aerial flights. Reynolds and his pilot tried to fly over West China by themselves, hoping to announce to the world that they had discovered the highest mountain on earth. But they got lost, the weather was bad, they saw nothing, and they were reprimanded by both the Chinese and American governments.

A few weeks later, Chinese pilot Moon Chen flew over the area and determined that the so-called "mystery mountain" the other pilots had seen was a completely different 24,000-foot peak. When he checked out Amni Machin, he found it was about 20,000 feet high. These were indeed very big mountains, but they did not compare in size to Mount Everest and its height of 29,028 feet.

In 1951, Brad was off again, this time leading the expedition that pioneered the West Buttress route on Mount McKinley. As he had predicted, the West Buttress was a safer, shorter route to the top than the way he climbed in 1942, or in 1947 when I was along. This time I stayed at home with the children and busied myself with community activities.

Two years later I was on my way to Alaska again. Brad had been working for years on the definitive map of Mount McKinley, but not even his three ascents of the mountain had given him all the information he needed. So in August 1953, he embarked on another expedition.

The children were off at summer camp for a month, so it was no problem for me to accompany Brad. The plan was to ascend two peaks in the Alaska Range—Mount Brooks, elevation 11,940 feet, and Scott Peak, elevation 8,800—and to conduct survey work from their summits. These were not major climbs in the sense that Mount McKinley was. The elevation above sea level was significant, and the Alaska snow and ice were factors, but the climbs were not terribly time-consuming. These weren't month-long sieges, but rather forays of a few days each.

Mount Brooks, located just a few miles east of McKinley, is a beautiful mountain that looks like the Matterhorn. Because it was much smaller than McKinley and didn't have much of a reputation, I imagined an easy climb. It turned out to be more of a challenge than I expected because of the deep snow on a long, steep ridge.

On our way to the summit, I was on the rope with Chan Waldron, who was from the education department at Brad's museum. We were sinking into the snow up to our knees with every step. I heard loud cuss words coming from above me, and it was obvious that Chan was tired and fed up. I shouted to Brad, "How much longer to reach the summit?"

Brad gave us a choice. He said we could immediately return to camp and come up again the next morning, or we could go on to the summit. But if we went to the summit, we would have to spend the night because Brad had to stay to complete surveying work on the top. My heart sank at the thought of climbing all this distance through deep snow again, so I voted to continue to the summit right then. After a brief rest, Chan agreed, and so did the fourth member of the group, Harvard student Ned Ames.

It didn't take much longer to reach the summit. The first thing we did was dig a snow cave. We didn't have any food or sleeping bags with us, and no tent, because we had expected this to be a day climb. Brad completed his survey work for the evening and that's when we realized how hungry we were. We soon realized, too, that it was going to be a long, miserable night. It got surprisingly cold. We sat on each other's laps and shivered so much that we could barely talk. Ned began shaking so hard his bones were rattling.

"We've got to give him something warm or he may not make it through the night," I said.

We searched frantically in our parka pockets and came up with an envelope of Kool-Aid and a few scraps of oatmeal that had fallen out of a food bag. Brad had a small Primus stove and an aluminum pot in his pack that he carried for emergency use. We cooked the scraps of oatmeal for Ned, and the rest of us drank hot Kool-Aid. This drink warmed me up and got me through the night.

The minute the sun came up we escaped the cave, like bears coming out of hibernation. But we couldn't descend right away. Brad had to finish his surveying and each of us took turns recording figures for him. The sun renewed our spirits, and our mood brightened. We realized how lucky we were to be in this magnificent spot with McKinley towering above us several miles away, its snowy summit glistening in the sunlight.

Then, from nowhere, a fighter plane screamed by and circled us, wobbling its wings. The pilot must have wondered what on earth four people were doing on top of Mount Brooks at dawn.

Going up Scott Peak was just a hike by comparison. Brad and his crew had already been to the top before I arrived in Alaska, but it had rained and they were unable to finish the surveying. They left the theodolite at the summit so that the instrument would be there when they returned. However, they underestimated how much it might snow, even in late summer. I accompanied them back to the summit, where we began to search for the theodolite. After an hour of probing and digging we still hadn't found it. Finally we struck something hard. We all shrieked "Thank God!" and dug it out.

Brad concentrated on his surveying as the rest of us got colder and colder. We jumped up and down to keep warm. My most vivid recollection of the brief time on Scott Peak was of a terrible headache and of suffering with it all the way down the mountain. My headache went away quickly, though, when I spotted a helicopter sitting on a knoll near the end of the glacier. It was waiting to whisk us back to park headquarters, to clean sheets and a hot bath.

Brad and I spent the rest of the month surveying for the McKinley map from each key point in the lowlands. We fought the weather and the mosquitoes all the time. Hot air rising from the tundra caused boiling in the air over the peaks, so most of the angles that we were determining in the survey were more accurate if we recorded them at dawn or in the evening. The mosquitoes were out in full force at those times.

The field work for the McKinley map was finally finished, and we returned home with a great sense of satisfaction. In the months that followed, Brad had to find a Swiss company that could produce the beautiful contouring and cliff-drawing required in creating the final map. It soon became obvious that the Swiss were still the world's masters of this skill. We made several trips to Europe while Brad was supervising progress on the map. The men who did the work had to have infinite patience and talent, and with Brad's insistence on accuracy they created a cartographic work of art—a map used by people around the world to get a true representation of this great mountain. It was published in the 1960s and is still the map most frequently used by those who climb McKinley.

We had a small cottage on the shore of Squam Lake in New Hampshire, and the next thing I knew we were making a chart of the lake! Brad wanted to determine the depth of the lake at three-hundred-foot intervals. We spent our weekends one summer tying Ping-Pong balls onto a fishing line, stretching the line across an area, and measuring the depth at every ball. Even the slightest breeze blew the line off course.

Another problem was trying to locate the big rocks beneath the water while sitting in our small motorboat. We put a stepladder in the boat so that Brad could sit on it and get a better view. This worked very well until the day our 10-year-old nephew was steering and made a sudden turn. Brad went sailing off into the water. He made an impressive splash.

We finally realized there was a better season to take our measurements: winter, when the lake was frozen. The positioning of the soundings would then be more accurate. To do this, we would drive a vehicle onto the ice, following a line surveyed across the lake. At intervals we would stop and punch a hole through the ice with an electric drill. We took depth measurements using a hundred-foot tape with a piece of lead pipe secured to the end. Brad would let the tape down into the hole until he felt it touch bottom, then record the depth of the lake at that spot.

We didn't let anything stop us. Once we accidentally put a jeep right through the ice, but with the use of a winch we pulled it back to shore. We drilled about 3,500 holes in the ice by the time we finished the map several years later, and the chart was soon in constant use by boaters.

During the lake-charting project, I remember sitting in the car with the children, reading the sad story of *Charlotte's Web* to them. We cried constantly. As the children got older, I taught them how to drive the car on the ice. This was a good opportunity to learn, because there was so much room out there—wide-open territory with lots of space to back up and practice turning.

No sooner had we finished the lake chart than Brad moved on to mapping the Squam Range, a popular area for hiking and camping. We enlisted the help of Harry Feldman of Boston, a professional surveyor who was a friend. He showed us how to use his Geodimeter, one of the first electronic, digital measuring machines.

The Squam Range project involved much hiking on rough, unused trails, plus lots of bushwhacking. Every once in a while when I got fed up with the bugs and the rocky trails, I would yell at Brad, telling him I hoped this would be the last of his crazy projects. He just kept plodding along ahead of me, never replying. He knew that after a good night's sleep I would be ready to go out with him again.

CHAPTER 16 *Sixteen*

MOTEL CAMPING

ONCE THE MAP OF THE SQUAM RANGE was finished, we made plans to take the children on a trip to see their country. The summer of 1958 seemed to be the right time. They were old enough to enjoy such a trip, but still young enough to want to be with us rather than off with their own friends and activities. Dotty was fourteen, Teddy was twelve, and Betsy was nine.

We wanted to turn them into fans of camping, so we planned to sleep in our tent and cook most of our own meals along the way. We didn't have a lot of money to spend, so we arranged to drive a new Plymouth station wagon across the country and deliver it to an agency in California. We were to pick up the car in Detroit. A friend of ours agreed to accompany us in our own car to Detroit and then drive it back to Boston.

On August 1 we piled into the car and headed west, with our neighbors waving and wishing us "Bon voyage" as if we were embarking on the adventure of our lives. In a way we were. We drove west into New York state in the midst of a heat wave and spent our first night in a field in Camillus, near Syracuse. It was a bad start. It was so terribly hot. Even though we all

◄ The occasion was daughter Dotty's debutante cotillion in 1960 when Brad and I took to the dance floor. *Photo by Bradford Bachrach*

got some sleep, by 5:00 a.m. the sun was beating down mercilessly on the tent roof and we were nearly expiring. We climbed out of our sleeping bags and went into a cafe for breakfast. Suddenly, Brad and I had a mutiny on our hands. The kids told us they never wanted to camp out again!

We explained that not all camping was like this. But as a treat, we promised to spend the next night in a motel. That was our undoing. The motel had a swimming pool and television. From then on they had no interest in camping. They insisted on staying in motels every night.

The irony of our change in plans did not escape me. The Washburns—who received so much publicity for climbing mountains in Alaska, for climbing Mount McKinley, for roughing it in the wilds—were camping out in motels. Worse yet, we enjoyed the comfort as much as the kids.

We drove about three hundred miles each day. The main challenge, as any parent knows, is to keep the kids from getting restless. The first major stop was a mill at the Ford Factory in Detroit, where molten steel was rolled out into long, thin strips to be used in the manufacture of automobiles. Then it was off to a Ford assembly line. A visit to Abraham Lincoln's birthplace in Springfield, Illinois, gave the children a sense of history.

We also stopped to visit friends in several places. One of our most exciting—or perhaps I should say terrifying—stops was in Wichita, Kansas, where our host owned a grain company. He invited us to ride to the top of a grain elevator, where vast quantities of grain were stored. We hopped on a step that was moving upward, and we soon approached the top. It was only then that I discovered to my great shock that the elevator simply continued on, dumping whatever was on it into the great mounds of grain in the huge storage bin below. We had to get off.

I screamed to the children, "Jump off at the top!" Thank heavens they did. We were still shaking when we got back down—by taking the stairs. To this day I can't imagine why our host didn't caution us about getting off at the top.

Although we had given up the notion of camping out, there were occasions when we couldn't find a motel. One night we drove until it was very late and then just pitched our tent in a field. The next morning we were almost blown away by huge trucks roaring past the tent. We discovered only then that we had camped in the middle of some uranium claims. Signs all over the place read "Keep out!"

The most adventurous thing we did on this trip was ride to the bottom of the Grand Canyon on mules. But there was a hitch. Betsy was only nine, and they had a rule that you had to be at least twelve years old to ride them. She began crying and was bathed in tears when Brad suggested the two of them hike instead. "Never mind, Betsy," he said, "we'll probably have more fun."

They filled their rucksacks with snacks and water, and late in the afternoon, to avoid the heat of the sun, they dropped over the edge on the South Kaibab Trail and soon disappeared in the shadow of the canyon. Betsy will tell you now that this several-hour walk was a high point in her life, a thrilling adventure. And one of the best parts was that she didn't have to walk back up. One of the mule packers who brought clean linen every day to the Phantom Ranch where we were staying was surprised to see that a little girl had hiked down.

"You're not going to make her walk out, are you?" he asked Brad.

Brad explained the situation.

"Oh heck, I'll take her out on a mule with the dirty linen and it will cost you only ten dollars." The deal was struck and Betsy had a ride back up to the rim the next day.

While Brad and Betsy were spending the night at the ranch, Dotty, Teddy, and I prepared to take mules down the next day, departing at dawn. None of us had much riding experience, so I was totally exhausted after the eight-hour ride down on muleback. Brad and Betsy were there to meet us and insisted that we jump right into the swimming pool to relax.

In spite of the discomfort, I would not have given up that trip for anything. I learned a lot about geology and plant life as we rode down through many different layers of the earth. The trip back to the rim the next day was equally fascinating and not as painful a ride. Little did I know then that I would soon be spending a great deal of time in the Grand Canyon.

As we drove into Las Vegas, Teddy pointed out the various hotels. He recognized them from television. We chose one that advertised all-you-can-eat breakfasts for a dollar-fifty. The children were ecstatic swimming in the pool. We wanted to teach the kids the evils of gambling, so we gave each of them a dollar to use in a slot machine and expected them to lose the money quickly. No sooner had Teddy put his first nickel into the machine than there was a loud clanking of change. He hit the jackpot! We tried to persuade him to quit while he was ahead, but the temptation was too great and he eventually lost everything. The girls made nothing to start with.

We wanted to drive through Death Valley on our way to Los Angeles, so we set the alarm for 4:00 a.m. to beat the heat. As Brad backed up the car in the early morning darkness, there was a loud bang. He had backed into a huge post and bent our car door. It could no longer be shut tight. We tried to regain our good spirits, but we drove out into Death Valley with some concern. We knew Death Valley was no place to have car trouble. At one point we passed a tiny pond, totally dried up, with a desiccated duck lying on the parched bottom. Brad and Teddy insisted on stopping the car in order to read a thermometer we had brought just for this purpose. The temperature was 120 degrees.

When we reached California, we delivered the station wagon to the agency. We were embarrassed to show them the broken door, but they laughed when they heard how it happened. While in Southern California we became one of the charter visitors to Disneyland, which had just opened that year. From there it was a ride on a fancy train up to San Francisco, then to the airport for the return to Boston.

No sooner had the five of us settled into our seats on the plane than an agent came down the aisle and whispered in Brad's ear. Brad turned to us and abruptly said, "Come on, we're getting out." Brad explained that the airline had oversold the flight and was willing to give us each a hundred dollars if we surrendered our seats and that we would be given a free flight to Boston later that night. While we were waiting, we sat next to a man who had just arrived from Australia and had also agreed to give up his seat.

"What a strange country this is," he said. "I have just arrived and the first thing that happens is they pay me money to get off the airplane."

That was our first experience with overbooking and we all hoped it would happen to us again soon.

It seemed like such a quick jump in time from our family trip across the United States until the children were traveling on their own. In 1964 our son, Teddy, was off to Tokyo—to compete in the Olympics. He was coxswain of Harvard's four-man rowing crew.

The Olympic opening ceremony was one of the most thrilling experiences of my life. The Japanese had organized everything beautifully, but no one had planned for the possibility that when hundreds of doves were released over the stadium, bird droppings would land on the heads of the athletes. Ted assured us it was not pleasant.

The crew finished fifth in the whole world, a magnificent accomplishment, but of course they were disappointed because they didn't win a medal. Teddy graduated from Harvard in 1965 and became a teacher of creative writing and coach of the freshman crew. Our daughter Dotty attended Smith College at first, then finished her degree at Boston University. Betsy earned her degree at the University of Washington.

Ted's great talent for crew was passed on in his family to his daughter Sally, one of our seven grandchildren. She became coxswain for the Brown University crew, which won a national championship race in 1994 and then headed for England to compete in the Henley Regatta. It would be a great event in her life, and we had to be there.

Ted had cautioned us that we should be prepared to dress up, but we didn't quite understand what that meant. Ted was very well-known in the racing community and we were given tickets in the steward's section, where everyone dresses elegantly.

Brad and I arrived at the steward's enclosure early on the morning of the Thames Challenge Cup finals and staked out two seats in the front row. About an hour before race time, an elegant appearing young woman pulled up a chair and placed it in the aisle next to me. We had been asked to keep the aisle clear for wheelchairs, so I asked her politely if she would mind moving her chair. She drew herself up importantly before lashing out at me.

"Never in all my years of coming to Henley has anyone ever told me where to put my chair," she yelled. "And what's more, certainly not an American!"

I couldn't think of any response except to say that we had been asked to keep the aisle clear. She began another tirade.

"I know the Americans have no taste, but imagine coming to Henley with a hat like yours! And I don't like your dress."

At this point I simply turned my back on her, but she kept on about how important her father had been in the Royal Air Force during World War II.

"I was in the American Air Force," Brad told her, "and if I remember correctly, we eventually helped save your lives. Without us you might be washing dishes in a German pub in downtown London."

About this time, Sally's race got under way. When her boat approached, three lengths ahead of the Cambridge University crew, we both yelled "Come on, Brown!" as loud as we could. I heard the woman exclaim, "Oh my god, they know somebody in the boat." She was apparently rooting for Cambridge, and our boat annihilated them. That was the last we heard from her.

The climax of our week in Henley was seeing Sally receive the Thames Challenge Cup, with her eight oarsmen standing behind her.

A couple of years after our cross-country family trip, I embarked on my own project by pursuing a course of study at Massachusetts General Hospital in Boston in the teaching of remedial reading. Dyslexia was being recognized more and more, and the language clinic in this hospital trained teachers to work with children who showed signs of learning disability.

At this period in education, many schools had done away with phonics. For a child with symptoms of dyslexia, this meant that reading and spelling were almost impossible. The Gillingham method, which I was taught, was based on phonics, so my pupils made significant progress in a short time.

I had pupils in several schools in the Boston area, but was soon asked to remain at the Shady Hill School, a private school in Cambridge. I started teaching there in 1964 and stayed for twenty years, helping many boys and girls before they went on to high school. It was extremely gratifying to watch their learning skills improve, and I felt this raised their self-esteem enormously.

I remember one little boy in the first grade who refused to take part in any classroom activities. When I asked him why he seemed so unhappy, he had such a heartbreaking answer: "I am so dumb. I can't read anything."

I told him that if he would let me help, I was sure that by the end of the school year he would be able to read. I will never forget the last day of school when his mother came to visit and I asked him to read a story we had been working on. He read slowly, but accurately, and when he finished, both his mother and I had tears streaming down our cheeks. He was so proud of himself.

I still meet former pupils who thank me for the help I was able to give them. Not many years ago, Brad and I were attending a reception at the Royal Geographic Society in London, and I noticed a young man hovering near us.

"Are you waiting to speak to my husband?" I asked him.

"No, Mrs. Washburn," he said. "I'm waiting to speak to you. You taught me in the fourth grade at Shady Hill when I couldn't read very well."

This student was now a banker in Europe, married to a lawyer, and obviously very successful. With a smile he said, "I don't have to spell very well now. I have a secretary."

Brad uses the surveying instrument as I take notes during one of our many days in the Grand Canyon as we worked to map this great landscape.

CHAPTER 17 *Seventeen*

THE GRAND CANYON

THE YEARS PASSED AND I WAS ENJOYING MY TEACHING. Our children were now grown and out of college and pretty much on their own. One day in the 1970s, however, I received a telephone call that upset my peace of mind. It was our old surveyor friend Harry Feldman, who had helped us long before on our New Hampshire projects.

"Hi, Barbara," he said. "I hear you're going to map the Grand Canyon."

I burst out laughing and said, "Where did you get such a ridiculous idea?"

"I'm serious," he replied. He told me he had been in contact with Brad. As he understood it, Brad and I would be going to the Grand Canyon soon to investigate the use of a helicopter on the project.

I hung up the telephone, completely astonished and not a little disturbed. Brad had said nothing to me whatsoever. I couldn't wait to confront him when he got home from work that night.

Brad admitted he had been afraid to tell me about his plans. But when he laid out the idea, it turned out to be more practical than I had expected. The project involved going to the Grand Canyon during the summer every year for several years to conduct map surveys. The trips would not compromise my teaching or disrupt my students' learning.

To begin the project we did have to find a helicopter and a good pilot. We would have to land on many of the buttes out in the canyon and make laser sightings from the top. For all of our flying in jets and in small planes, and Brad's aerial photography, neither of us had much experience with helicopters. We eventually settled on a helicopter company that provided a pilot who had flown hundreds of hours in Vietnam. Betsy, then teaching school in Denver, joined us on the initial scouting mission. One day she said to us, "You know, this canyon is not just a place, it is a religious experience."

A hotel room served as our studio here as we worked on the map we were making of the Grand Canyon during part of the 1970s.

The mapmaking was to begin with a helicopter landing on Zoroaster's Throne, one of the highest buttes in Grand Canyon. From there we would be able to see many of the other spots we needed to land on. As we got ready to take off on the flight, I suggested to the pilot that he might want to change his footwear. He was wearing patent-leather shoes. I knew there might be snow on Zoroaster's Throne, so Betsy, Brad, and I were wearing our L.L. Bean boots. But the pilot was scornful of the suggestion.

"We never make forced landings," he said.

Famous last words.

The pilot headed straight for Zoroaster's Throne, then descended steeply. We landed with a big bump. The door flew open abruptly and Brad shouted, "Jump out quickly!"

The helicopter tail was gyrating crazily. The pilot had misjudged the wind and had lost control on landing. He smashed the tail rotor on the only juniper bush on the butte, and we could go nowhere without a tail rotor. Despite Brad's climbing background and my experience in Alaska we were in no position to climb down. It would have taken a champion rock climber and lots of rope to descend the cliffs of Zoroaster's Throne.

While Brad and the pilot were studying the situation, I said to Betsy, "Let's go sit and dangle our feet over the edge and enjoy this marvelous scenery." As we started to walk toward the edge, the pilot let out a scream. When I asked him what was wrong, he said, "I'm terrified of heights."

Brad said it looked as if we would have to radio the office for another helicopter.

"The radio doesn't work," the pilot said.

That shocked Brad. He asked, "Well, do you have any tools? Maybe we can fix it."

The pilot carried no tools.

Brad pulled his Swiss Army knife out of his pocket. Fiddling with buttons and tightening screws, he got the radio working. But no one answered our call at the helicopter office.

We resisted the idea of sending out an SOS. We didn't want the entire Air Force looking for us. As a way around this, Brad sent out a CQ signal. That simply means, "Anyone listening? Please give us a call on this frequency."

Soon we had a response from an airliner that was nearing Flagstaff, Arizona. Brad asked the pilot to call Grand Canyon Helicopters and suggest to them that they give us a call on their radio. Thank heavens they did this, but it was a humiliating experience—because Grand Canyon Helicopters wasn't our helicopter company. It was the competition—the company we hadn't hired.

Still, these people sent a helicopter to rescue us. The damaged helicopter sat alone atop Zoroaster's Throne for two weeks before it was flown off with a new tail rotor. Our pilot, Vietnam experience or not, neglected to tell us he had never before landed on a butte. We remained friends with him, but we never flew with him again.

Over the next three years we made 697 helicopter landings, some of them on very precarious perches. As we made more and more landings, we became very good at the game. Brad became adept at leaping out of a helicopter while it hovered above the ground. I preferred to wait until it touched down. We made thirteen two- or three-week trips to the Grand Canyon for this project. The National Geographic Society financed the work, and we accomplished it under budget, which always pleased them.

We had a lot of adventures along the way. One of our earliest difficulties involved a trip into the canyon in a blizzard. You might think of Arizona as a land of perpetual sunshine and dry desert landscape, but it does snow. We were on an exploratory trek to set up a survey station at the Phantom Ranch at the bottom of the canyon. It was February, and there was deep snow on the canyon rim. As we dropped over the rim on the South Kaibab Trail, with the snow up to our waists, Betsy and I began to giggle. We just

▶ From the top of Dana Butte in the Grand Canyon, we took sightings as part of our map work during the early 1970s.

couldn't imagine that we were going to get very far. But Brad, with his usual determination, assured us that the situation would improve as we hiked lower.

He was correct. As we descended, it got warmer, there was less snow, and by the time we reached the river, there was no snow at all. But before we hit the river, we met a hiker heading upward—a Frenchman carrying a briefcase and wearing patent-leather shoes. He had no idea he was hiking upward toward a blizzard on the rim, and he didn't seem to understand what we were trying to tell him. Farther down the trail we used an emergency phone to alert the Park Service to be on the lookout for this misguided hiker. The rangers never saw him, so we can only assume he got out safely.

When we knocked on the door of the Phantom Ranch late in the afternoon, there was no answer. We banged much louder and the caretaker finally opened the door.

"Where in hell did you people come from?" he wanted to know "The canyon has been closed all day. No one is allowed on the trails."

That was news to us. We told him we didn't know the trails were closed. And we explained that the deep snow didn't present much of a problem for us after our Alaska experiences. He took pity on us and gave us a good meal and a cabin. The next day we were lifted out by helicopter.

During the course of the mapping project, I walked down every important trail several times—but I always managed to get a helicopter ride back out. There were days when we walked at the bottom of the canyon in temperatures as high as 114 degrees.

"How much farther?" I would yell to Brad, and his reply was always the same:

"We're almost there."

Brad once smashed his nose on a rock when he tripped getting out of the helicopter. He was clutching the laser prisms in his arms and refused to let go, so he couldn't break his fall. Meanwhile I was atop a butte three miles away, waiting for a radio go-ahead from Brad to take measurements to the prisms. Instead, the helicopter appeared and landed beside me. "Don't worry," the pilot said. "Brad is OK. I just left him at the hospital. He wants me to take you to him."

Brad looked horrible. The bleeding was stopped by shoving lengths of bandage tape into his nostrils and almost down his throat. Needless to say, he was uncomfortable. He had two bad days, but on the third day the doctor was scheduled to remove the bandages. However, while we were in our bedroom, waiting to return to the hospital, Brad suddenly began pulling yards of bloody tape out of his throat.

I almost fainted because it looked as if he were pulling out his intestines. Then I realized he was doing this because the tape had gotten stuck down his throat and he was choking. It looked like a magician pulling miles of scarves out of his mouth. After recovering from the shock of the scene, we both began laughing hysterically. We called the doctor to tell him Brad had taken care of the removal job by himself.

Many volunteers helped us with our work in the Grand Canyon. We sent them down the canyon trails with measuring wheels and then compared their results with ours. The distances pretty much matched, so we felt we came up with reasonably accurate measurements for each trail.

John Noble Wilford, a science writer for *The New York Times*, asked to interview us. We told him he couldn't really understand what we were doing unless he walked the trails with us. So he did. He became so intrigued with cartography that he later wrote a successful book called *The Mapmakers*—the story of the pioneers in this discipline from antiquity to the space age.

Our map was published in 1978 and a copy was inserted into the July issue of *National Geographic* magazine and sent to all 11 million members. Brad and I felt this had been our most fascinating project because the Grand Canyon is such an inspiring place to work. There were moments I thought I would die of heat and fatigue, but now I look back on the Grand Canyon and realize that Betsy was right: Being there is a religious experience.

As soon as we finished the Grand Canyon map I knew that Brad would come up with some adventurous new project. I was immersed in my teaching and

Brad was overwhelmed with fund-raising for the museum, but one day he came home and mentioned that we had been invited on an African safari as the guests of Roy Little, the founder of Textron Company.

The moment I heard the word *Africa* I jumped for joy. I had always wanted to see the marvelous animals of that continent. Brad, however, started giving me reasons why he couldn't go. February was his busiest time at the museum—and he wasn't terribly interested in taking pictures of animals. I quickly pointed out that I had always gone with him to Alaska. Now it was his turn to go with me where I most wanted to go. He relented. And now he agrees that this was the best trip ever. As it turned out, Brad was ecstatic photographing animals and birds in their natural habitat.

This was the last of the old-fashioned safaris in Kenya, with thirty-two native bearers taking care of eight of us. Our guide was Sid Downey, a long-time Africa expert who had been guiding Princess Elizabeth when she was told her father had died and she was now Queen of England. We went out in a jeep every day and Downey located animals for us to observe and photograph. On the first day, we saw a lion kill a gazelle and the scene horrified us—but then we realized this was simply how animals survive in the wild. It was also gruesome to watch wild dogs surround a gazelle and tear it to pieces. It seemed cruel in our eyes, but at the same time it was impressive to watch the pack operate as a unit.

The high point of the trip was flying to the camp in Tanzania where Jane Goodall was studying chimpanzees. Childhood memories of watching monkeys in their cages at a zoo in Boston came flooding back as we visited the camp and I was able to observe the chimps she had befriended. One day I was sitting with Jane in an area where the chimps came to play, when a female chimp named Flo wandered in with her baby. Jane told me to sit very quietly. Flo sat down on a rock and just stared at me. I sat and stared back. Suddenly the baby jumped out of Flo's lap, ran over to me, and poked me, and then ran back to hide in her mother's lap. The act was so like that of a human child.

A few minutes later a large male chimp appeared. Jane warned me to sit really still because he was at the stage of life where he needed to establish dominance. He looked at me, beat his chest a few times, and then jumped onto a large rubber tire hanging from a tree and began to swing, just as any child would have done. (Brad said the actions of the male chimp reminded him of members of the Boston City Council.)

When Jane and I left this area, we encountered a large baboon on the trail. I was petrified because the animal, about my size, stopped right in front of me and acted as if it might jump up on me and hug me. It didn't, but it did show a keen interest in my brightly colored skirt. The baboon circled me, pulling on the skirt and feeling it. When it finally left me alone and ambled off down the trail, I was trembling.

After the chimp research camp, we visited the Serengeti Plain in Tanzania. As we approached the area, Sid Downey handed us the binoculars and said, "Have a look." Brad and I thought we were seeing heat waves in the distance, but the shimmering turned out to be thousands of zebras and wildebeests migrating across the plain. Our jeep moved slowly into this wall of moving animals, which simply parted, the animals paying no attention to us. Every once in a while, a female wildebeest would drop a newborn baby and give it a slight kick to make it stand up. Then the little creature would have to keep moving with the crowd.

We will never forget the sight of all those animals, because it was as if we had turned the clock back thousands of years. We hated to leave Africa, but our safari came to an end and we had responsibilities awaiting us at home.

CHAPTER 18 *Eighteen*
A MAP OF EVEREST

BRAD DECIDED THAT HE WOULD RETIRE by the time he turned seventy—a decision that set in motion one of our biggest adventures, the effort to map Mount Everest. He retired as director of Boston's Museum of Science in May 1980, the month before his seventieth birthday. Among the gifts at his retirement party were two round-trip tickets to Nepal—from museum staff members who had heard him say many times that before he died, he would like to be carried in a sedan chair to a spot above Darjeeling where he could view Mount Everest.

The tickets to Nepal inspired Brad to carry out one of his dreams. He was now too old to climb Everest, but he was not too old to fly over it and map it from the air. Brad contacted his friend Bob Bates, who had been director of the Peace Corps in Nepal—and had also been the chaperone of the young future king of Nepal when he came incognito to study at Harvard. We had met this young man when he visited Brad's museum, and now that he was king we hoped he would remember us and would give us permission to fly over Everest. Brad wrote to him and the king replied with an encouraging letter.

About that time, Brad received an invitation to lecture at the Institute of Glaciology in Lanzhou, China. This seemed like a good opportunity to stop off in Nepal to check into getting permission to fly over Everest. Of course, given Everest's location on the border of Nepal and Tibet, we would need permission not only from Nepal, but also from China for any activity in Tibet.

We took off on this new adventure with a feeling of great excitement. As our plane approached Kathmandu in Nepal, I had the impression of arriving in a very mysterious place. The hills were terraced for crop-growing, and tiny villages perched high on the hillsides. Thank goodness Bob Bates and his wife were at the airport to meet us, because going through customs was chaotic. And we were overwhelmed by hordes of small boys trying to carry our baggage to make a few cents.

In the confusion of getting a taxi and traveling to our hotel, Brad lost his camera. He bought an excellent replacement at a store in the city, which was surprisingly well-stocked. But then we remembered seeing many Nepalese boys with cameras around their necks. The cameras were doubt-less purchased in Bangkok or Hong Kong and resold in Nepal. It also crossed our minds that Brad may have been looking into buying his own pilfered camera.

After settling into our hotel, we took a walk around the town to learn about stupas, the dome-shaped mounds or towers that serve as Buddhist shrines, and to get a general feel for the place. My first impression was of crowds of people, terrible traffic, and loud, high-pitched automobile horns. The taxi drivers play chicken, constantly scooting between cars and swerving around the sacred cows that wander the streets. I was shocked by the piles of debris and garbage in the marketplace, and I found it difficult to sleep because of the barking dogs that roamed outside all night.

It was time to turn our attention to the purpose of our visit to Nepal—obtaining permission to fly over Everest. We had to deal with a Mr. Basnyat, the surveyor general. He had an office on a balcony surrounding a huge, open courtyard, where cows grazed on trash and where groups of Nepalese men hung out. A court of law also was situated on this balcony, and on our visits to Mr. Basnyat we often saw defendants in handcuffs and chains.

We climbed several flights of stairs to reach the office, where we were greeted by three men in white tunics who alerted Mr. Basnyat. Soon his office door opened and we were invited in. We were served tea immediately. Mr. Basnyat was very cordial and spoke English well enough for us to understand him. He listened intently to our proposal, but it soon became apparent that he did not have the authority to grant us the permission we needed. Our proposal had to be presented to the National Planning Council, which included the Military Department—and these officials could not understand why we would want to make a map of Mount Everest. They were suspicious of our motives.

After many, many meetings, and countless cups of tea, we were told that if we could get approval from the Chinese to fly over Everest, then the Nepalese, too, would grant permission. Of course, they thought the Chinese would never let us do it.

The time for Brad's lectures in China was fast-approaching, but we had been stalling for time because he didn't feel well. However, we knew we had to honor his commitment, so we left Nepal for China. Bob Bates and his wife waved goodbye to us as I shouted to them, "I don't know what's going to happen to us, but we're on our way!"

What happened next was totally unexpected. As we were landing at Guangzhou Airport, I got ready to show my passport. To my horror I couldn't find it. I frantically searched my pockets and my handbag, on the floor, and on the seat of the plane. As we headed toward the exit of the plane, I looked plaintively at Brad and whispered, "I can't find my passport."

I expected his immediate reaction to be, "How could you do such a stupid thing?"

He may have been thinking that, but he didn't say it. He was silent, and while we were wondering what our next move should be, a Chinese student came up to us and said, "Is your name Washburn? I am to be your guide while you are here." He was a representative of China's Academy of Science.

The guide was stunned when Brad told him I didn't have my passport with me. We had to calm him down. Brad took over. He asked the airline to telephone the Hong Kong airport, where I had showed the passport before boarding the plane to Guangzhou. It wasn't there. Brad then asked our guide to take him to the American consulate, where he would try to get a new passport for me.

But meanwhile I was to be held hostage at the airport, with two armed guards standing behind me. They did not let me out of their sight, even following me to the ladies' room. As I waited for word from Brad, I kept busy by reading *Space,* one of James Michener's long books. Reading kept me occupied, but it didn't keep me warm in the frigid November air of the unheated airport.

At the consulate, Brad was told that securing a replacement passport would take at least a couple of days. Brad was undaunted. "What do you need in the way of information," he calmly asked. The consul needed my birth certificate, which Brad was carrying in his pocket. He also needed three pictures of me, and Brad pulled these out of his wallet. The consul issued the passport immediately.

The whole process took only three hours, but when I saw Brad enter the waiting room to liberate me from my guards, I burst into tears. I felt as if I had just been released from jail. We thanked the guards and headed for the hotel, both of us a little shaken.

The lobby of our hotel in Guangzhou displayed a beautiful waterfall, so I assumed our room would be very attractive. Wrong. It was very simple, though adequate. After an unappealing dinner, we were told by a British man who joined our table that the flight to Lanzhou would be a tough one, crowded and uncomfortable. Brad already was feeling under the weather, and the thought of a miserable flight just made matters worse.

"Tell the guide I'm sick and am in no condition to fly today," he told me.

When I relayed this message, the guide paled and said, "You have to go. All arrangements have been made. There are no other flights."

After much persuading from me, Brad faced up to the flight. Our British dinner companion was absolutely correct. It was a miserable trip. We were in a Russian-made airplane with no food served all day. Vegetables and live chickens in huge fish-net bags clogged the aisles. On two occasions a flight attendant came by carrying a tray, raising our hopes of receiving a meal. The first time, she offered us a piece of hard candy. On the second trip down the aisle, she offered small combs for our use.

Our foodless eight-hour trip brought us exhausted to Lanzhou Airport, where we were met by a tall and friendly scientist, Wang Wenying, from the Institute of Glaciology. During the drive to our hotel, he kept looking at me, then bursting into laughter. He would giggle, then laugh out loud again. What could possibly be so hilarious? I noticed that there was a picture of me in a book he held in his lap. I guessed that seeing me in person instead of as just a name and photo had somehow set him off. In any case, he turned out to be a sweet and helpful man.

We were deposited at a spartan hotel that had been built, I believe, by the Russians, at a time when there was no real interest in tourism. Entering the cold, barren hotel dining room the next morning, it looked as if we were the only guests. Then I heard a voice from a distant part of the dining room, around a corner:

"What in the world are you doing here, Barbara?"

The voice belonged to Maynard Miller, a geologist from Idaho that Brad and I knew very well. Maynard had been on my first Alaska expedition, in 1940, when we climbed Mount Bertha. He was then a Harvard freshman and I was a new bride. Now a professor, he was in China to give some lectures.

For our next surprise, Brad and I had to face up to the breakfast on our plates. It consisted of a saucer of peanuts and a bowl of cold spinach soaked in vinegar. We didn't quite know how to cope with the situation, because we didn't want to offend our hosts. We finally mustered the courage to ask, in a whisper, for some bread. We also quietly asked if it was possible to obtain an egg. In two minutes these items were placed before us. For the rest of our trip, we asked for the same thing and our breakfasts became much more satisfying.

The scientists at the Institute of Glaciology showed great pride as they displayed their maps and explained their work on the glaciers of Tibet. Brad asked why they were so interested in mapping glaciers. Their reply surprised us, though it shouldn't have. Glaciers were the only source of fresh water in Tibet, so it was very important to know which were advancing and which were retreating. They told Brad he could keep any one of the maps that were on display, but they withdrew the offer when he chose the one of Mount Everest's north side, saying, "Oh, I'm sorry, but that one is secret."

Dr. Shi Yafeng, the director of the institute, had met Brad more than three decades earlier when Brad came to China to research the height of Amni Machin. Shi Yafeng had been a young student then, and he always referred to Brad in his letters as "my most honorable professor." I had great admiration for the people at the institute. In very cold weather they traveled long distances to their jobs on bicycles or in trucks. There was no heat in the building, so we held conferences huddled together in our heavy coats.

The climax of our visit to Lanzhou was a surprise birthday party for me, with a dinner and a beautiful birthday cake. We were happy to find the meal pleasing to our palates, with no octopus tentacles or other delicacies we were not accustomed to. Brad is a great adventurer when it comes to visiting places, but he is not adventurous with food. I struggle to eat almost anything, but Brad's treats occasionally wind up on the floor under the table. After this touching party, we bid farewell to our friends and withdrew to the hotel to pack for our departure the next day for a flight to Xian, China.

When we came down to the hotel lobby in the morning we found Wang Wenying waiting for us. That dear man rode his bicycle for miles in the dark and cold, over four inches of fresh snow, to bid us goodbye. He handed Brad a rolled-up newspaper, with instructions to look inside it on the plane.

"You'll find good reading," he said.

Inside the newspaper was the secret Chinese map of Mount Everest that Brad coveted!

CHAPTER *Nineteen*

TOURISTS WITH A PURPOSE

IN XIAN WE WERE MET BY A BIOLOGY student who did his best to show us the sights of the city despite our inability to speak each other's language. He took us to view the life-size terra cotta statues of warriors that had recently been excavated. We also climbed seven stories up in an ancient pagoda to look down on the city, and ended the afternoon with a visit to the Hua Ching Palace Museum.

As we approached our hotel, our hearts sank. It was another of those enormous, gray, dreary buildings built by the Russians. We had a large suite with high ceilings and no heat. The bathroom floor was covered in water from leaky pipes, and cockroaches floated on the surface. We wore our L.L. Bean boots anytime we had to use the bathroom.

We were taken on a drive into the countryside the next morning, through an area of huge cabbage patches and cotton fields. The road was lined with thirty-foot-tall poplars and willows. We saw thousands of bicycles and trucks and old-fashioned carts, with both men and women hauling every conceivable item, from vegetables, cotton, and furniture, to oxygen cylinders and steel bars.

We left on the train for the city of Wuhan the following evening. We decided to explore the train a bit, which turned out to be a mistake. We walked by the open door of the kitchen in the dining car, and the scene was one of raw meat and blood all over the floor. We decided to skip dinner altogether. Our sustenance for the trip would be the peanuts we carried as emergency rations.

But soon a knock came at our compartment door. There stood a young conductor, inviting us to come to dinner. We refused. She insisted. We gritted our teeth and followed her to the dining car, where much to our surprise, we had a delicious meal of fish, many different vegetables, and soup. But the whole time I was eating, I kept thinking back to the bloody scene on the kitchen floor.

Our train stopped at every tiny town along the way. The countryside was flat, with a succession of fields, some green, some brown. As dusk came, we saw workers heading homeward along narrow paths between cultivated fields and their huts of mud and brick. This trip gave us a feel for the vastness of this great country.

There was a small dinner party in our honor at Wuhan University, a science and technology school where Brad showed slides of the mapping of the Grand Canyon. We were awakened early the next morning by rousing martial music from loudspeakers in the middle of the campus—apparently the university's alarm clock.

While Brad toured the photogrammetry department, I visited a kinder-garten. Adorable children sang songs and recited verses for me. In the day-care nursery were tiny babies in rows of bassinets, watched over by a stern-looking woman. I couldn't resist telling her that when my babies were that age, they were at home with me. She offered no response—and of course I didn't mention that I had once left my children behind in order to climb Mount McKinley.

The next stop was Beijing, where we landed at the new airport and received a bit of good news: During the following day, Sunday, we would be on our own. Chinese trips tend to be heavily scheduled, especially official visits, so we were happy for the free time. Brad took me to see the Temple of Heaven, which he had seen in 1948 and felt was the most beautiful building in China. When I saw it, I had to agree.

Brad noticed many changes from the China of more than thirty years before. The city was cleaner, but unfortunately it was spreading out, with many Russian-designed, boxy, gray buildings. There were no private cars on the street—only trucks, buses, bicycles, and hordes of pedestrians. No more was everyone wearing dark blue robes. The men now wore trousers, and the women were dressed in bright colors.

We spent a warm and windless day at the section of the Great Wall of China forty miles from Beijing. We were awestruck by the wall's size and the quality of the workmanship, as well as the incredible steepness of the slopes that the wall traverses. We also visited the Ming Tombs, dating back to the fifteenth century. Our visit to the famous marble boat built by the Empress Dowager at the Summer Palace on Kunming Lake was quite a disappointment. The lake level was way down, and the boat, covered in dust, was resting on mud. At the Beijing zoo, the tigers, monkeys, and giant pandas stole the show.

While we were in Beijing, we received a telegram from Nepal saying that the government there appeared ready to grant our request for the Everest flight. Brad was ecstatic and proceeded to give a scheduled lecture at the Chinese Institute of Geography in a relaxed frame of mind. After the event, one listener told Brad that his talk was "the best scientific presentation I've ever heard from anyone in my life."

We were also busy trying to get permission from the Chinese government. We looked for help from the Nepalese embassy, where Dr. Yadunath Khanal was the new ambassador to China. We had already met him in Kathmandu, and he seemed to favor our project.

Shortly before our return flight to Kathmandu, Dr. Khanal invited us to his home for dinner. His wife was a sweet, shy lady who I'm sure would have preferred being home in Nepal rather than serving as an ambassador's wife in China. After dinner, just as we were saying good night, Dr. Khanal said to Brad with a twinkle in his eye, "You have your permission." The Chinese government had approved our request. Brad and I were astonished and said in unison, "But how did you get it?"

"Don't ask me," he said. And we never did. To this day we wonder how he got the Chinese to grant us permission to fly an airplane over Mount Everest.

We were very grateful, but knew that we still had to work with the Nepalese government because their consent was not yet in writing. With our hopes high, it was time to return to Nepal and see if we might have the same good fortune that we found in China.

We stopped in Hong Kong, where we were invited to Thanksgiving dinner at the home of a U.S. naval attaché we had met earlier in China. Before we left for the dinner, Brad made quite a discovery. He was in the bathroom, and I heard an exclamation from him. He soon emerged, with a guilty expression on his face. After a moment of hesitation, he confessed he had found my missing passport in his hip pocket. He had been sitting on it all the way across China.

At the dinner party, another surprise awaited. A guest at the dinner was the American consul from Guangzhou, the man who approved the new passport for me while I was being guarded at the airport. We returned my original passport to him and we were all convulsed with laughter as we told the crazy story.

Our flight back to Kathmandu on a crystal-clear day was especially thrilling for Brad because he was able to pick out some of the highest mountains in the world: Kanchenjunga, Makalu, and Everest. Mount Everest looked dark and sharp, towering behind the beautiful white pyramid of Makalu. I said to Brad that Everest didn't hold a candle to Mount McKinley in appearance. A lady in the front of the plane who knew I had climbed McKinley stood up when we got our first view of Everest and said, "Barbara, it's very disappointing." I felt she was blaming me for Everest not being more presentable.

In Kathmandu we were now destined to attend many more meetings, each with its required cups of tea. We talked with all the people in different departments of the government who might help advance our Everest mapping project. Brad was finally told to write a proposal that could be presented to the Cabinet. We felt optimistic, because the Nepalese officials didn't say "no." And they insinuated "maybe."

We left on December 6 for a very long flight to Zurich. Switzerland gave us a deep feeling of relaxation. We could safely drink the water, and we weren't confronted with all the pollution and overcrowding. The language barrier largely disappeared, since many of the people we were seeing spoke English, and Brad and I spoke French. We met with Swiss cartographers, the best in the world, and made plans for the Everest map, contingent on Nepalese approval. If Brad could obtain the aerial photographs of Everest, the cartographers would make the map.

When we arrived at last back home in Boston, all we wanted to do at first was sleep. But we were soon into our normal routines again, more or less. I was still teaching, and Brad went every day to the office he continued to maintain at the Museum of Science, even though he was officially retired. We still didn't know for sure if the mapping of Mount Everest was in the cards.

During the first few months of 1982, Brad wrote out one draft after another of an agreement on mapping Mount Everest and sent them to Mr. Basnyat, the surveyor general of Nepal. One day Brad received a letter from the King of Nepal approving the project—but stating that the details would have to be worked out "with the concerned officers" of the Nepalese government. This turned out to be the mapping subcommittee of the National Planning Council. So in November we headed off once again to Nepal to pursue negotiations. We also made some reconnaissance flights to study the weather and technical problems related to the proposed operation.

During one of these flights, we had a real scare. On a cloudless morning, just as we were approaching the spot where I thought Brad would at last be able to get a good picture of Mount Everest, the plane shuddered, flew straight up, and nearly flipped over. Brad, sitting by the open door in preparation for taking pictures, was hanging on for dear life. I peeked at the ground and wondered how much it was going to hurt when we crashed. And I recalled a remark made to me one day by a colleague at my school:

"Barbara, you will surely die a violent death because of the kind of life you are leading."

In moments, the pilot regained control of the plane and Brad yelled "Let's get the hell out of here!" It was discouraging, because it had seemed as if this was going to be our lucky day to get good shots of Everest. Then we realized it *was* our lucky day because the pilot had been able to keep the plane under control even after hitting a violent "wind shear."

Brad worked each day on the proposed agreement with Nepal, and each day Mr. Basnyat made changes, sometimes only one word, sometimes a whole sentence. We got the impression he was stalling for time. Christmas was approaching, but we felt that we couldn't go home for the holidays— that if we left Kathmandu, nothing would ever happen. We had Christmas dinner at the home of the American ambassador, meeting other guests from all over the world.

We then learned that our Chinese permission for the flight would expire in just a few days, on January 1, 1983. Brad had just submitted the tenth draft of the agreement to Mr. Basnyat. We decided to go home, and with a feeling of hopelessness we left for Boston.

CHAPTER 20

'SOMETHING TERRIBLE'

BRAD DOES NOT GIVE UP EASILY. He continued to rewrite proposals, sending them off to Nepal. On February 7, 1984, we received what we had been waiting for—approval from the National Planning Council of Nepal. Brad signed the agreement immediately and returned it. It was the fifteenth draft. The Chinese permission had long since expired, of course. But five months later, the Chinese agreed to extend their approval.

We still didn't have financing for the project, and we had to move fast. Brad contacted the National Geographic Society, and the organization swiftly authorized $75,000 for aerial photographs. That was only half of the amount needed, however, but the museum loaned us the rest. Feverishly we made plans. On October 11, we ate at a Chinese restaurant and Brad's fortune cookie read, "Life for you is a dashing and bold adventure."

The next day we flew out of Boston, met in Seattle with National Geographic photographer Bill Thompson, who would be joining us in Nepal, then continued on toward Bangkok. We made it to Bangkok, but our luggage didn't—all ten pieces and 450 pounds, including cameras and film. We had to make an on-the-spot decision to either go on without our stuff or stay and wait for it. We went on. In Nepal we waited it out at the airport and miraculously everything showed up. Who knows what route it followed?

Our biggest baggage battle was yet to come. Brad presented a letter from the royal palace stating we did not have to pay import duty because we were a scientific expedition. The chief customs officer, a formidable looking character, stared at Brad and said, "The king is not authorized to write a letter of this sort." It took days of effort in a bleak customs office, and piles of paperwork, to free up the gear.

The logistical problems in Nepal were endless. Nepal observes an enormous number of holidays, and it seemed that every time we needed a job done, it was a holiday. The pilot we considered to be the best was fired by the government and we had to hire him separately. We needed passes to land the Learjet that we had secured from a company in Sweden, and to obtain these we had to negotiate with the airport manager, a rude man who subjected us to a torrent of abuse. He wanted to know why we wished to engage in such an expensive, useless project. He made insulting remarks about my relationship with Brad, and I had to firmly inform him that we had been married for more than forty years. Justifying his obstructionism, this man explained that they did things differently in Nepal. We were well aware of that.

Other parts of the project were progressing well. The Learjet was flown from Sweden to Switzerland and the mapping equipment was flight-tested. Key members of the aerial mapping team were due to arrive soon in Kathmandu, including Werner Altherr from Swissair Photo-Surveys and photographer Bill Thompson.

I began to feel ill. I tried to keep going because I didn't want to miss any of the action in Nepal, but I had to keep taking aspirin to hold my temperature down. Secretly I was terribly worried about the crisis I would create if I became seriously ill. November 10, 1984, was my seventieth birthday, and American friends of ours in Kathmandu were throwing a party for me. At the last minute I told Brad to go on without me.

My fever rose to 104 degrees and Brad began to panic. He called for a doctor, who arrived in my room still wearing his motorcycle helmet. The doctor left with several vials of my blood, which he put in a rucksack on the back of his motorcycle. As miserable as I felt, I burst out laughing at the image of my blood dripping onto the streets of Kathmandu as he sped along.

Things got worse. A trip to a medical clinic revealed that my white blood cell count was very high. This prompted the American doctor there to treat me for several different tropical diseases. When none of these medicines worked, he sent me out for X-rays. The X-ray equipment was obsolete by American standards and a lead protector was never used. I began to think I might die of cancer from the radiation from so many X-rays, none of which revealed anything.

Various doctors who were guests at the hotel took a crack at diagnosing my problem, but I continued to run a high fever. A Nepalese lady brought me some pomegranates and told me that if I ate the seeds, I would get better. A Nepalese doctor urged Brad to take me to Bangkok for better treatment. Brad was frantic. We packed toothbrushes and pajamas, but nothing else because it never occurred to us we wouldn't return to Nepal. I was so weak that Brad pushed me in a wheelchair through the airport. We arrived at the Bangkok Nursing Home in the middle of the night, my first time in a hospital since my last child was born in 1946. I was frightened, but when I was tucked into bed by a lovely Thai nurse, a wonderful feeling of relief came over me.

I was given a bronchioscopy, where my throat was frozen and a long tube was pushed down into my lungs. They put a blindfold over my eyes and I willed myself not to cough. Next I had a bone marrow test. I was laid on my stomach and a large needle was inserted into my back. I had test after test, but no one was solving my problem and I was growing weaker.

Eventually the doctors concluded that I had lymphoma. They did not inform me of this. They told Brad, saying that if he wanted me to be able to die at home, we should leave for Boston immediately. Brad did not tell me what the doctors had told him. He simply said we were going home to Boston. I was relieved, but my first thought was that I had to wash my hair, that I couldn't arrive home looking ill and disheveled. Gathering all my strength, I took a shower and tried to set my hair. I nearly fainted, but I was too proud to ask for help.

Brad alerted the National Geographic Society to the situation, and they assigned Barry Bishop to fill in for Brad as director of the Everest project. Bishop, one of the first Americans to climb Mount Everest and the holder of a Ph.D. in Nepalese studies, already was in general charge of National Geographic research projects. The photo mapping of Everest would continue without us.

When the hospital staffers in Bangkok said goodbye to me, they were really saying farewell and hoping I would make it home alive. We left for the airport in an ambulance. It was the Christmas season and flights were mobbed. Brad confessed that we didn't have seats, but we were at the head of the waiting list. We could only pray that two people wouldn't show up. God was good to us. There were two single seats, and a flight attendant and two kind passengers worked it out so Brad and I could sit together.

I dozed much of the time while Brad kept an eye on me. Then someone said the words *caviar* and *lobster*, whereupon I sat bolt upright and said, "I'll have some." I was not feeling better, but I figured that I might as well enjoy these treats. All of a sudden I felt like eating—even though I still had a high fever and a bad cough and my lungs were filled with fluid.

I was beginning to guess I might have a fatal illness. I even began musing about the woman Brad should marry if I died. I mulled over a list of widowed friends and I couldn't think of a single one who would fit Brad's requirements in a wife. I decided I had to concentrate on getting well.

When we landed in Boston, our children and grandchildren were waiting for me. I was taken off the plane on a stretcher and put into an ambulance. My little granddaughter Sally ran up to the stretcher and handed me her favorite stuffed animal.

At Massachusetts General Hospital testing began anew. The doctors decided I did not have lymphoma. However, one doctor told Brad they were pretty sure I was dying of *something*. "She doesn't have cancer," the doctor told him. "She has something terrible, but we don't know what."

The kidney biopsy was the worst test. I had to lie absolutely still on my back for eight hours. A hard pillow was placed against my kidney, causing a miserable backache. I read a book on meditation and tried to concentrate on something else, but that didn't work. I asked if I could turn over to relieve the pain, but the nurse directed me to remain on my back for the full eight hours. The next morning I told the doctor how painful the test had been.

"Why didn't you ask the nurse for some medication?" he asked. No one had ever suggested I could do that.

The kidney biopsy gave us the answer: I had Wegener's granulomatosis, a rare blood disease. Once a fatal disease, it had become treatable. I was given large doses of prednisone, a steroid, eighty milligrams at a time, and another powerful medication, Cytoxan, directed at this disease. I took my medication faithfully for four years and recovered fully. I was released from the hospital on Christmas Eve 1984.

The phone rang at 7:00 a.m. on Christmas Day. It was Werner Altherr of Swissair Photo-Surveys.

"Merry Christmas from the team in Kathmandu," he said. "I am holding in my hand a small packet of pictures, ten inches square and three inches thick, worth $150,000. These are the pictures from our flights over Everest. They are perfect. We send our love."

Some months later Brad and I received an exciting invitation. The king and queen of Nepal were coming to the United States and we were asked to a state dinner at the White House in their honor. We met President Reagan and Nancy Reagan, and I was seated at a table for eight, with Barbara Bush, the vice president's wife, as our hostess. I had a gentleman on each side of me, but no clue as to who they were. I expected Mrs. Bush to introduce us, but she spoke only to the man beside her.

In desperation I turned to the gentleman on my left and said, "What do you do and why are you here?"

"I am Kenneth Dam," he replied. "I am assistant secretary of state and I am in charge of this evening's dinner because the secretary of state is in the Far East."

I blushed with embarrassment, but he saved the day with a generous smile. The gentleman on my right, who was in the television industry, was equally charming. President Reagan was a witty host. He said he had spent a wonderful day with the king and only wished he could have spent as agreeable a day with the Democratic House Speaker, Tip O'Neill.

Comedienne Joan Rivers and weatherman Willard Scott were seated nearby. Two pianists entertained, and the Marine band played dance tunes of the 1930s. Brad and I found ourselves dancing beside the Reagans, terrified lest we bump into them.

After mapping Mount McKinley and the Grand Canyon, a survey of the Presidential Range in New Hampshire brought me and Brad much closer to our home in Boston. Here we're at work on the project in 1980. *Photo by Jamie Cope*

CHAPTER 21
Twenty-One
AUDIENCE WITH THE KING

THE COMBINATION OF MY SLOW RECOVERY from illness and my age led me to retire from teaching, and I missed it. But Brad always had projects in the works. We were now busy mapping the entire Presidential Range in New Hampshire. We shot our laser beam from station to station, as we had done in the Grand Canyon. Occasionally we used a helicopter to cover the distances. When we landed on the summit of Mount Isolation, a group of angry climbers accused us of ruining the wilderness with noise pollution.

My job was to accurately record all the angles that Brad reported as he read his instrument. Then I had to do a simple calculation to tell him whether his measurements were correct. I hated it when the angles were off, because it meant we had to take the measurements all over again. It seemed I was always either standing around freezing or being devoured by mosquitoes. One time when I was sitting on top of 6,288-foot Mount Washington, I was so cold I thought of sabotaging the project by giving Brad an incorrect figure. I resisted the temptation.

We also had to measure the trails, which involved walking all of them. Many volunteers helped us. Casey Hodgdon, who was from New Hampshire and worked for the Forest Service, knew all the trails by heart and was a wonderful companion. Casey always made sure I was OK, and he and other helpers kept track of me by radio when I was out on my own. Sometimes

I met hikers who thought it strange for an elderly woman to be walking alone, carrying a radio.

It took some time for Brad and me to recover from the shock of my illness and our disappointment at not flying in the Learjet for the photography over Mount Everest. But now we had to come up with the rest of the financing needed to complete the map. The final contouring and artwork would be a long and expensive undertaking.

The people at the National Geographic Society contacted Brad one day with the news that they would pay the entire cost. They wanted to publish the map in the centennial issue of their magazine. Euphoric, Brad set the mapmakers in Switzerland to work. We traveled to Zurich every few months to check on progress of this truly international project. Representatives of seven different nationalities were at work on the map.

Brad and I, along with Werner Altherr of Swiss Airphoto, were on hand at the printing plant in New Jersey in October 1988 as the map come off the press at the rate of 20,000 copies an hour. At one point Brad and Werner thought the color green was slightly off in one corner. Assuming it would be a major undertaking to fix it, they still mentioned it to the production manager. "No problem," he said. He pushed a button and corrected the detail.

The press ran day and night. It took nineteen tons of ink to print the map. Six carloads of paper were used, more than a million pounds in all. The National Geographic Society printed 11 million copies for its members. All the maps laid end-to-end would have reached from San Francisco to New York and back again

We had promised to present the first copy of the map to the King of Nepal. I was still weak from my illness, but I didn't want to miss the fun, so I insisted on going back to Nepal with Brad, Werner, and his wife, Heidi. On the day of our audience, however, the king's secretary said the monarch was tired and would see only Brad. Severely disappointed, we gave Brad permission to fight for us. He reminded the king's secretary that the four of us had come a long way for this special occasion and that we would take only a few minutes of the king's time—and that it should be all of us or none of us. The secretary relented.

We were with the king for a delightful half hour. He asked many questions about the map, and he permitted a filmmaker with the public television program *NOVA* to record the occasion. In a brief personal conversation with the king, I was asked to remember him to one of his Harvard professors.

Brad and I went from Nepal to China, where we presented the Everest map to representatives of the Chinese Academy of Science. The Chinese Mountaineering Association threw a dinner party for us, with a thirteen-course dinner that included several items we couldn't identify. I tried everything, but when I was told I was eating sea slugs, they stuck in my throat. Brad managed to drop his on the floor. The fish was good, but the head was still on and the eye seemed to be looking right through me. One of the climbers said he was the leader of the first Chinese expedition to reach the summit of Everest. He told us that the difficulty of the climb had nearly made them turn back, but that they continued on for the glory of Mao.

I appreciated that I had led an exciting, adventurous life. But as I grew older, it seemed that more and more people also began to think that way. Not only did there seem to be more articles in newspapers and magazines about Brad and me, but we began receiving different kinds of awards.

In 1978 I received a medal for special achievement from my high school, Girls Latin School, which was celebrating its 100th anniversary. A year later Brad and I were awarded the Gold Medal of The Royal Scottish Geographical Society for "outstanding contributions to cartographic research." In Edinburgh and Glasgow, Brad gave lectures on mapping the Grand Canyon. My only duty was to smile sweetly and say "thank you." We then jointly received the first Alexander Graham Bell Award of the National Geographic Society for "unique and notable contributions to the science of geography through exploration and discovery over more than four decades. . . ."

In 1980 I received a medal from my alma mater, Smith College. The day I got the letter asking me to accept the Smith College Medal was traumatic. It was the same day my daughter Dotty told me she was separating from her husband. I was utterly devastated and I burst into tears, moaning to myself that I couldn't possibly accept the medal because I must have been a bad mother. After I cried myself out, I eventually realized it was not my fault that my child's marriage did not work out.

The medal was presented to me on February 20, 1980, and the citation read, in part:

> *Barbara Polk Washburn, Class of 1935. Explorer, mountaineer, cartographer, teacher of the handicapped. You were the first woman to climb Mount McKinley, and since 1940 your physical endurance and trained scientist's eye have made you a distinguished contributor to the team effort which surveyed and mapped Mount McKinley and the Grand Canyon. . . . You have been one of the key strategists and fundraisers of the team which raised the money and planned the building and equipment of Boston's magnificent Museum of Science. . . . You were, as well, a devoted volunteer fundraiser for Boston's Hospital for Women, the Boston Children's Service Association, and for your alma mater. You have also built another career of service as a teacher of remedial reading. . . . Smith College is proud to recognize your achievements and to award you a Smith College Medal.*

The most exciting honor of all came to Brad and me in November 1988 when we received the Centennial Award of the National Geographic Society for "an illustrious career of mountaineering, exploring, mapping and museum administration." Fourteen hundred guests attended the Washington, D.C., dinner to honor us and the other recipients of the award, including Sir Edmund Hillary, Jacques Cousteau, Mary and Richard Leakey, Jane Goodall, and John Glenn.

Brad and I led the procession of medal winners to the head table. When the Navy band struck up a rousing tune and I looked out at the sea of faces turned to us, I was overwhelmed. However, when I saw my daughter Betsy's smile filled with emotion and pride, I pulled myself together and led the group up the stairs onto the platform. I sat between Ed Hillary and John Glenn. Ed was a good friend and I found him easy to talk with, but John did not seem able to make small talk. As a United States senator, he had a politician's manner more than an astronaut's.

President-elect George Bush gave a brief speech and then shook hands with each of the recipients. When he greeted me, I said, "I wish you good luck." He said, "I'm going to need it."

Brad and I walked across the platform to receive our award while scenes from our expeditions were shown on a huge screen. As Brad stepped to the podium to speak for both of us, President Gilbert Grosvenor of the National Geographic Society placed a beautiful Steuben glass globe in my hands.

"It's very heavy," I whispered. "I don't know if I can hold it."

"Don't drop it," Gil said. "It cost $6,000."

Each recipient also received a check, to be presented in turn to non-profit organizations. Brad and I divided our $10,000 four ways, making donations to the Massachusetts General Hospital, which saved my life; to Recording for the Blind, where I do volunteer reading; to Boston's Museum of Science; and to the North Conway Institute, which helps people with alcoholism and troubles with the law. After all our years of fund raising and asking others for money, it was a real thrill to be able to make a gift.

Several years later Brad and I flew to St. Moritz, Switzerland, for presentation of the King Albert Medal, which honors a former king of Belgium who was a noted mountaineer. The medal was awarded at this ceremony to three people: Brad; Sir John Hunt, leader of the British expedition that in 1953 made the first ascent of Mount Everest; and posthumously to a brilliant Polish climber who lost her life on Kangchenjunga.

For the ceremony in a castle, we were asked to remove our shoes in order to protect the invaluable needlepoint carpet on the floor. As we sat down, John Hunt whispered to me, "Barbara, I have a hole in my sock."

"Never mind, John, no one will notice," I assured him. I don't think anyone did.

Chapter 22
Twenty-Two
A SHIMMERING LIGHT ON EVEREST

MOUNT EVEREST CALLED US BACK AGAIN. Brad had recovered well from some tough health sieges—an aortic aneurysm followed by a triple heart bypass operation—and he was itching to take on another project. Now he wanted to determine the precise height of Everest. The tallest mountain on Earth is listed as being 29,028 feet high, but Brad wanted to find out if it had been pushed even higher by the movement of the earth's tectonic plates.

In the spring of 1992 we returned to Nepal. We weren't sure how we would react to the altitude. When we were younger and climbed mountains in Alaska, we had plenty of time to acclimatize because the expeditions lasted a long time. Now that we were older, we planned to fly by helicopter directly to 12,000 feet, to a hotel above the Sherpa community of Namche Bazar. We felt fine when we arrived, but took care to move around slowly for a couple of days.

Brad and I and Nepalese surveyor Amir Shakya, who was working with us, were the only guests in the hotel. In bed I fended off some of the cold and damp of the hotel with the help of a hot water bottle. The spectacular view from the grassy patio outside our bedroom made up for the discomfort. We were surrounded by snow-covered mountains, with Mount Everest at the center of the view.

We soon became accustomed to the daily schedule. Every morning at six, a young man knocked on the door and gave us a bucket of water for flushing the toilet. A short time later he returned with a kettle of warm water for bathing. At the signal for breakfast, we put on our parkas and entered the dining room. The only heat in the hotel came from a large, open fireplace that seemed to function only in the evening. We would sit by it, hunched over, trying to read from its limited light.

The plan was for us to take a laser sight on prisms that were to be placed on the summit by a climbing team led by Vern Tejas. Brad tried to make the laser sight each day, but we had no direct communication with the team and no way of knowing if the climbers had yet reached the summit. We were simply waiting to see the shimmering red light from the prisms. Finally we decided it would be best to return to Kathmandu and try to find out if they had reached the summit. We couldn't communicate with the helicopter from the hotel, so we had to walk down a couple of miles to Namche Bazar.

On the way, we walked into what looked like a small Sherpa inn. Suddenly a handsome Sherpa boy threw his arms around me and kissed me. I was taken aback, but he quickly said, "Don't you remember me? I'm the young deaf boy you met in Talkeetna, Alaska, who was going to try to climb Mount McKinley. We had lunch together." We were amazed to see him. He had been part of a group of handicapped young people who attempted to climb Mount McKinley but were turned back by terrible weather.

We took a room at the inn, and as soon as we were settled, Brad went to work setting up a survey station that others could use in the future for Everest observations. I sat in the sun for a while, but a sore throat that had started on the walk from our hotel got worse and I began to run a fever and to shiver. Finally I went to my room and snuggled into my sleeping bag. I told Brad I just wanted to sleep.

A couple of hours later, the door opened and a Japanese lady carrying a black bag came in. It took me a moment to figure out she was a doctor. Our host at the inn had run half a mile to find her. The first thing she said was, "Open your mouth and stick out your tongue." I tried to do it, but I was laughing too hard. In a line, behind her, were all the inn's employees, and maybe the neighbors too, opening their mouths and sticking out their tongues. They had gathered to see what was going on. The diagnosis was tonsillitis and the doctor gave me antibiotics.

I felt better in the morning, but everyone was worried that I wouldn't have the strength to climb the steep hill to the helicopter landing spot. These kind people built a stretcher with a beautiful Nepalese rug on it and were going to carry me. When I assured them I could walk, one man said he had a horse I could use. That idea scared me, so I just started walking. A woman insisted on holding my arm. We made it up the hill and I found a place to stretch out and rest. The woman offered me some food that she fried on a stove, including one item that turned out to be sheep entrails. I rubbed my head and stomach to show her I was too sick to eat.

While we waited for the helicopter, I wanted desperately to visit the famous town of Namche Bazar, a steep half-mile below the helipad. Brad took my arm to steady me and off we went. The town was, indeed, a real bazaar, with just about everything for sale. I bought a Snickers bar to help get me back up that steep hill. I was so happy to finally board the helicopter, and I gave profuse thanks to the pilot, a fellow who looked like Omar Sharif.

Back in Kathmandu, Brad learned that our team of climbers was at high camp waiting out the weather. He then returned to Namche Bazar to prepare for another summit sight while I stayed in the city and took care of my illness, which turned out to be strep throat. When Brad returned ten days later he had exciting news. One day at 4:00 a.m. he and surveyor Amir Shakya aimed a laser beam at Mount Everest and saw the shimmering red light. The climbing team had placed the prisms at the summit, and the beam struck the prisms. Amir made the initial sight because Brad wanted a Napali to have the thrill of taking the first measurement.

This measurement represented a first step in a year-long process of determining the mountain's true height, which had long been pegged at

29,028 feet. This eventually led to a new internationally accepted GPS altitude for Mount Everest of 8,850 meters, or 29,035 feet.

We returned from the journey to Nepal with a feeling of great accomplishment and the expectation of staying home for a while, but the summer of 1993 saw us back in Alaska. The Anchorage Museum of History and Art was celebrating its twenty-fifth anniversary and asked Brad to put on a slide show.

While we were in Anchorage, ABC-TV's *Good Morning America* flew us to the Ruth Glacier on the south side of Mount McKinley to interview us. The glacier provides a picturesque view of McKinley—but the mountain was shrouded in clouds the whole time. We were surprised how many small planes were flying around the area. How incredible it was to think that this once-remote area of the Alaska Range was now the focus of so much traffic.

The show also wanted footage of Brad taking aerial photos as he hung out the open door of a plane—something he had done for many years. The show's cameramen flew in a plane behind the plane carrying Brad, and they got shots of him—now at age eighty-three—sitting in the open door with his fifty-pound camera in his lap, every so often hanging out to get a picture.

After this trip I began to think our travels were over. But in November 1993, Brad and I were invited by Grand Circle Travel Company on a cruise to Antarctica. Brad agreed to present several lectures to the other passengers during the trip, and I was also scheduled to give a talk.

We left Miami two days after Christmas for a night flight to Punta Arenas in southern Chile, and found our old friend Norman Vaughan there. Incredibly, he was planning to climb Mount Vaughan, the mountain in Antarctica named decades earlier in his honor. He made it to the top when he was eighty-nine years old.

We boarded a German cruise boat that accommodated four hundred passengers and to our delight, Sir Edmund Hillary was aboard as one of the lecturers. The ship worked its way southeastward out of the channels that surround the southern tip of South America. We then emerged into the southern Atlantic and swung southwestward, finally reaching Cape Horn. Heavy winds and huge waves caused the ship to roll relentlessly, and many of the passengers took to their beds. Brad and I, armed with seasickness pills, managed very well.

By the time I was scheduled to give my talk, the wind had subsided and the sea had calmed. It was a kind of afternoon tea, with an audience mainly of women. I talked about meeting Brad, our first adventures, the conflict I had over leaving the children, and our later adventures, spread over more than fifty years.

The beauty of Antarctica is indescribable. Snowy mountains and glaciers were not new to me and Brad; they reminded us of Alaska. But there was a feeling of peacefulness and remoteness amidst the icebergs that I had never experienced before. We talked about the great courage and skill of the early explorers who brought sailing ships through this area.

Our cruise also included a stop at the Falkland Islands to visit the nesting grounds of penguins and albatrosses. Our final stop was Buenos Aires for a scheduled two days of sightseeing, but Brad had a scheme. The city of Mendoza, only an hour's flight away, was close to Aconcagua, highest mountain in the western hemisphere. At 22,841 feet, it stood about 2,500 feet higher than Mount McKinley. Brad had talked long before of climbing Aconcagua with me, but the trip never materialized. Now he simply wanted to see it.

We flew to Mendoza, where we contacted a couple whose names had been given to us by a friend. Over dinner, the husband said his son could drive us to Aconcagua. So early the next morning, the son and his girlfriend picked us up for the thrilling—I should say scary—150-mile ride to where climbers begin their ascent of the mountain.

We traveled a very winding road and our young driver went at great speed, caressing his girlfriend all the way while Brad and I slid back and forth on the rear seat. As we came around a corner we had our first view of Aconcagua. It appeared to be such a high peak that I must admit to a great sense of relief that I was too old to climb it. We walked a short way up the trail and were amazed at the large number of climbers who were heading toward the summit. This climb is so easy that Vern Tejas once pushed a bicycle to the top and rode it down!

We returned to Buenos Aires from our side trip just in time for the cruise group's final party, a barbecue on a ranch owned by an Argentine couple. The main house resembled the Palace of Versailles, and the horses and gardens were equally impressive. We dined on the famous Argentine beef, which Brad and I (in whispers, of course) agreed was a bit on the tough side. However, it was definitely a superb meal compared with many we have had on our adventures.

Brad and I were at the University of Alaska Fairbanks when this photo was taken in 1990.

Twenty-Three

THE VIEW INTO HEAVEN

WE RETURNED HOME FOR A WHILE but I began to get restless. When our daughter Betsy called one day in 1994 inviting us to go to Alaska with her family, I jumped at the chance. It was wonderful for once to be just plain tourists in Alaska and to have fun with the children and the grandchildren. Betsy wanted the grandparents along for Bradford, who was twelve, and Heather, who was four. We took a boat trip across Prince William Sound to show them the glaciers. We visited the main oil terminal at Valdez, and our grandson was excited to see the site of the *Exxon Valdez* oil spill of 1989, which had been discussed at his school.

Our time in Talkeetna, where climbers gather to prepare for the ascent of Mount McKinley, was the high point of the trip. We all flew to the Ruth Glacier and landed on the snow, with McKinley rising 15,000 feet above us. The kids thought the mountain was awesome.

Brad showed some slides while we were in Talkeetna, and it seemed as if everyone in town showed up. It was quite a revelation for our grandchildren, who really hadn't understood that their grandfather (and their grandmother, too) had gained some fame in Alaska. And they had never heard him give a public talk or seen pictures of what we did in Alaska.

People kept coming up to the table while we were eating, asking for our autographs. The children's eyes got bigger and bigger. A tourist, sitting behind us and observing this scene, handed Brad a piece of paper torn off the menu, and said to him, "I don't know who the hell you are, but please sign this and I'll find out tomorrow."

Just before Christmas 1994, I received a letter informing me that the University of Alaska Fairbanks would like to bestow on me an honorary degree of Doctor of Science. I felt at first that I should not accept because I was not in any way a scientist; I was only Brad's assistant. But the university insisted, pointing out that I had done much cartography work. Finally I began to look forward to the honor—ready to consider it my reward for all the days and nights of either freezing or sweating that I had endured at the top of North America and at the bottom of the Grand Canyon.

May 7, 1995, was hot in Fairbanks, with students at the university lying on the grass, basking in the sun. Commencement exercises were held in a huge gym on campus, where I reported to a young lady who helped me put on my robe and hat. Since I stand only a bit over five feet tall, I was sure the robe would be too long, but the length seemed manageable and the mortarboard stayed on my head with the help of a few bobby pins. In the procession, I walked between the president of the board of regents and the president of the University of Alaska system, both well over six feet tall. As it turned out, my robe was indeed a bit long and I came close to stumbling over it a few times, but my escorts grabbed my arm before I fell.

The citation that was read at the ceremony said the honorary degree was presented to me in recognition of what it called my "pioneering spirit, dedicated work in mapping and surveying throughout the world" and "continued devotion to children and the handicapped." I had felt that I didn't really deserve an honorary degree like this. But when I heard the citation read, I suddenly felt very proud. I even had the thought, "Maybe it's OK. Perhaps I do deserve it."

When I got back home, I went to an appointment with my hairdresser and I was greeted with, "Good morning, Dr. Washburn." I wanted to look around to see who she was talking to. But it's true that the ceremony in

Fairbanks meant I was now Dr. Washburn. It also meant there were now two Dr. Washburns in the family.

One day in 1996, I was back in academic garments. Boston University bestowed a joint honorary Doctor of Science degree on Brad and me. What a surprise: That made me a double doctor.

Over the next couple of years, Brad spent a great deal of time in again researching—and again proving false—the old claim made by Dr. Frederick Cook that he was the first person to climb Mount McKinley. This controversy has flared off and on for decades. Brad has shown by charts, maps, research, and photographs that there is no way Cook's claim that he climbed the mountain in 1906 could be true.

We traveled to Fairbanks to participate in a mock trial on the issue, but after all their public statements and all their attacks on Brad, Cook's adherents refused to participate. Two Fairbanks judges declared Cook's claim to be a fake.

We were back in Alaska in 1997 for an event commemorating the fiftieth anniversary of my ascent of Mount McKinley. On June 6, I found myself in Talkeetna to reminisce about that great trip. Brad and I visited the new national park ranger station, which was displaying paintings that George Browne made during the 1947 climb. Earl Norris, our dog driver from that expedition, came by to visit.

In Talkeetna I reminded people that it wasn't really my ambition to be the first woman to climb Mount McKinley. It just happened: I was an accidental mountaineer. The ranger station also was showing photos from the expedition. There was one of me and Brad at the very top, wrapped in our parkas. And once again I remembered the view of Alaska from the summit—how much it did seem like looking out at heaven.

In May 1999, Brad and I were installed as charter members of the Alaska Climbers Hall of Fame. The hall of fame is housed in the Talkeetna Alaskan Lodge, with a spectacular view of Mount McKinley from the back deck. Brad joked about his age, telling the crowd that at eighty-eight he was just a shadow of the climber he once was. As for me, I was greatly honored to be included, at the age of eighty-four, with a select group of mountaineers like Ray Genet, Hudson Stuck, Walter Harper, and Harry Karstens. Brad likes to say that at our age, we are living at the "cutting edge of the twilight of life."

I've had more than my share of luck, both in the mountains and in my family life. I rode out that tough nine-day storm on Mount McKinley and managed to return safely to my children. When I agreed to Brad's marriage proposal more than sixty years ago, great luck was again with me. I could not know then that he would become such a loving and devoted husband and caring father to our children. Nor could I anticipate that he would lead me into such an exciting life.

My children sometimes tell me that I led "Dad's life." That is true—but what a fool I would have been to go my own way and miss all of those adventures. I was very lucky to have a husband who wanted me to share his life and who constantly gave me credit for what I did. He opened up a whole new world for me.

However, I received two letters a while back that gave me as much satisfaction as any adventure. The letters were from two men who were students of mine at the Shady Hill School twenty-five years earlier. They saw a newspaper article that praised Brad's accomplishments, and they both said they wanted the world to know I had accomplished something very special for them. They said that without my help, they would not have made such a success of their lives.

When I went off to college my father said to me, "I don't think I need to worry about you, because you seem to have a lot of common sense."

Maybe so, but I've also had a lot of good luck along the way.

INDEX

About Lew Freedman

LEW FREEDMAN IS A SPORTS/ADVENTURE WRITER for the *Chicago Tribune* and former sports editor of the *Anchorage Daily News*. Author of more than a dozen books about Alaska, Freedman has worked frequently on stories with Barbara and Brad Washburn over the past decade.

Freedman has won numerous journalism awards in a career that has included work at newspapers in Pennsylvania, Florida, New York, and Alaska. A graduate of Boston University, he earned a master's degree from Alaska Pacific University.

Freedman and his wife, Donna, have a daughter, Abby.

About Barbara Washburn

BARBARA POLK WASHBURN WAS BORN IN 1914. A graduate of Smith College, she married museum director, mountaineer, and cartographer Bradford Washburn on April 27, 1940. One month later Brad asked her to accompany him on a mapping expedition in Alaska.

Despite having no mountaineering experience, Barbara became part of climbing teams that made first ascents of Mount Bertha and Mount Hayes in 1940–41. Six years later, she became the first woman to reach the summit of 20,320-foot Mount McKinley, North America's highest peak.

When she was not climbing, exploring, or mapping with her husband, Barbara, the mother of three, became one of the nation's earliest remedial reading teachers and worked at Shady Hill School for more than twenty years. She has received many awards recognizing achievements in several fields of endeavor.

At 86, Barbara was still traveling, mostly to accept the many awards and honors bestowed upon her and her husband. The couple makes their home in Lexington, Massachusetts.

CPSIA information can be obtained
at www.ICGtesting.com
Printed in the USA
FSOW03n1306200415
6498FS